Forbidden Narratives

Volume 1

Hippocrates' Latin American Legacy: Humoral Medicine in the New World

George M. Foster

Volume 2

Forbidden Narratives: Critical Autobiography as Social Science

Kathryn Church

Forbidden Narratives

Critical Autobiography as Social Science

Kathryn Church

University of Toronto
Ontario, Canada

Gordon and Breach Publishers

Australia China France Germany India Japan Luxembourg
Malaysia The Netherlands Russia Singapore Switzerland
Thailand United Kingdom United States

3 Boulevard Royal
L-2449 Luxembourg

British Library Cataloguing in Publication Data

Church, Kathryn
   Forbidden Narratives:Critical
   Autobiography as Social Science. -
   (Theory & Practice in Medical
   Anthropology & International Health;
   Vol.2)
   I. Title II. Series
   362.22

   ISBN   2-88449-212-7   (hardcover)
          2-88449-213-5   (softcover)

For Ross

who also survived . . .

The sociological imagination enables us to grasp history and biography and the relations between the two within society. That is its task and its promise. . . . No social study that does not come back to the problems of biography, of history and of their intersections within a society has completed its intellectual journey.

C.W. Mills, *The Sociological Imagination*

Those of us who have also, in the course of our sojourn in the kingdom of the sick, endured the initiation rituals of biomedicine and had its meanings incised literally (not merely inscribed metaphorically) into our flesh, are the twice-born . . . those likeliest to question received wisdom from any source.

Susan DiGiacomo, "Metaphor as Illness"

This book doesn't want to wallow in the individualized recollections of the personal-memoir kind of writing, or search for the true self in the inner recesses of the personal psyche. Instead it wants to attack critically the dichotomies, divisions, separate categories that split the personal from the social. It sees as an urgent part of this process of redefinition the attempt to cut through the warping dualisms of subjectivity/objectivity, personal/social, masculine/feminine.

David Jackson, *Unmasking Masculinity*

CONTENTS

INTRODUCTION TO THE SERIES

Theory and Practice in Medical Anthropology and International Health seeks to promote works of direct relevance to anthropologically informed international health issues, practice, and policy. It aims to bridge medical anthropology — both biological and cultural — with international public health, social medicine, and sociomedical sciences. The series' theoretical scope is intentionally flexible, incorporating the most current advances in social science theory, while its topical breadth ranges from specific issues to contemporary debates to practical applications informed by current anthropological theory. The distinguishing characteristic of this new series is its emphasis on cultural aspects of medicine and their links to larger social contexts and concrete applicability of the anthropological endeavor.

PREFACE

Forbidden Narratives: Critical Autobiography as Social Science explores overlapping layers of voices and stories which convey the social relations of psychiatric survivor participation within the community mental health service system in Ontario, Canada. Perhaps its most unique feature is that it begins with tales of the personal and professional changes which I have gone through in relation to psychiatric survivors over the past decade. Writing myself into the book in this way gives it a "survivor frame." This is a key feature which is supported by feminist theory. The work then shifts to stories about psychiatric survivor participation in the implementation of community mental health system reform by the Ontario government. My account of this process attempts to portray the unpredictable character of policy making as it is lived by the thinking, feeling people who actually do it.

All of these stories demonstrate ways in which the knowledge/power relations of community mental health are significantly disrupted by processes which bring forward survivor knowledge repertoires. When this happens, mental health professionals and bureaucrats become unsettled; their personal as well as professional identities are called into question. The emotional expression of this "unsettlement" is an integral part of policy re/formation; the supposedly rational practices of planning also mobilize emotional investments, desires, and pain. The book thus takes up the subjective dimensions of power and the disunity of state order.

ACKNOWLEDGMENTS

I am grateful to Susan DiGiacomo for taking an interest in the manuscript I sent to her simply out of a desire to connect, for seeing it through to this form, and for her warm personal support. Libbet Crandon-Malamud read and commented on a draft in great detail and with welcome enthusiasm at a time when she was quite ill. We never met but I remember her with great respect.

There are a number of people who are explicitly named in this text and I thank them for allowing this sometimes difficult exposure as a contribution to my intellectual project: two amazing psychiatric survivor leaders, Pat Capponi and David Reville; the ever-brilliant "Survivors of Sociology," Jane Haddad, Michelynn Lafleche, Kate McKenna, and Sharon Rosenberg; a great doctoral supervisor, David Livingstone; my wonderful parents, Stuart and Lorraine Church; my intrepid partner, Ross Gray. As well, I am indebted to all of the people I interviewed for chapters 6 and 7, who spoke with remarkable frankness about their experiences of policy making.

CHAPTER 1

Beginning from 'I'

She entered the story knowing she would emerge from it feeling she had been immersed in the lives of others, in plots that stretched back twenty years, her body full of sentences and moments, as if awaking from sleep with a heaviness caused by unremembered dreams.

Michael Ondaatje, *The English Patient*

I left Saskatchewan in 1983. Ross, my partner, had been accepted into a doctoral program at the Ontario Institute for Studies in Education (OISE) in Toronto. Our uprooting left me unemployed; I gave up a job as a Master's level psychologist working with young children and families. My attempts to find similar work in my new home were unsuccessful. Instead, through personal connections, I secured a research contract with the national office of the Canadian Mental Health Association (CMHA). For the next four years I was involved in the struggle to establish "consumer participation" as a policy of the organization. Consumer participation in the community mental health field is generally understood to mean establishing and/or increasing representation by "consumers" or "survivors" of psychiatric services within the system's decision-making bodies (e.g., boards of local agencies, regional health councils, provincial committees).[1,2] Doing this work within the CMHA brought me into contact with psychiatric consumers/survivors for the first time. This is where I entered the story.

In 1989 I became a doctoral student in sociology at OISE. I was driven by a desire to understand more about psychiatric survivor participation in making mental health policy. The most profound lesson of my return to university is captured in these words by C.W. Mills:

the most admirable thinkers within the scholarly community ... do not split
their work from their lives. They seem to take both too seriously to allow
such dissociation, and they want to use each for the enrichment of the
other.... What this means is that you must learn to use your life experience
in your intellectual work. (1959: 195, 196)

My doctoral research began with persistent, nagging, frustrating, burning
questions about my own practice first as a mental health organizer and then
as a researcher. It called upon all my life experience as I was initiated into
the complexities of the psychiatric survivor movement. Guided by two
prominent survivors, I spent three years observing, documenting and organizing support for several notable survivor projects. I also researched how
"consumer participation" was and was not enacted by a government-ap-
pointed committee investigating the possibilities for community mental
health services legislation in Ontario. As part of this exercise, the legislation
committee hosted a province-wide public consultation to which consum-
ers/survivors were specifically invited.

These engagements gave rise to two significant outcomes. First, my
research acquired theory — specifically, strong threads of feminist poststructuralism (Weedon, 1987; Lather, 1991).[3] As I went along, I critically appropriated fragments of theory which illuminated my practical dilemmas. Indeed, I became fascinated with continually-coming-into-theory as an aspect
of academic work which I wanted to reveal rather than mask in my writing.
Secondly, the relationships which I formed with psychiatric survivors over
the course of events had a remarkable effect: they cracked me open as a
person. In seeking to understand survivor pain and politics, I plunged
headlong into my own. Right in the middle of my research I experienced a
physical and emotional breakdown. What was I to make of this unprecedented personal eruption?

Breaking down prompted me to take up "consumer participation" at the
intersections of "public issues of social structure" and "personal troubles of
milieu" (Mills, 1959: 226). I perceived connections between my collapse and
the difficulties which mental health professionals experienced during the
legislation consultation. I detected a pattern. Professionals confronted with
"consumer" knowledge repertoires become upset; their personal as well as
professional identities are called into question. The disruption is expressed
emotionally, with feelings ranging from discomfort to frustration to tears.
There is anger which is out of proportion to the situation; there is silence
when there should be speech. I discovered emotions as an unpredictable and
disruptive feature of policy-making. Gradually, I came to understand "consumer participation" not as representation but as an "unsettling relation"
(Bannerji et al, 1991).

These discoveries were unexpected and they presented me with a dilemma. To be true to my own experience and analysis, I would have to write an account of my project which expressed its personal and emotional dimensions. In so doing, I would have to confront ways in which academia itself is compartmentalized: the "public" is split from the "private," the "personal/subjective" from the "rational" (Rockhill, 1987; Bowles and Gintis, 1987; Zola, 1991; McKenna, 1991).[4,5] This book articulates my struggles with this problem over a period of several years. The story has parallel threads. It traces my (be)coming into feminism and my politicization around issues of "health" and "health care" simultaneous with the (be)coming of psychiatric "consumers" through speaking, writing and participation in public roles/functions. The form I use for this exploration is what Jackson (1990) refers to as "critical autobiography."

Critical autobiography gives me permission to do something which academics rarely do: write myself into my own work as a major character. This plunge into the autobiographical is (also) unexpected. I fully intended to be "objective" about my work with psychiatric survivors but the realities of genuine engagement made it virtually impossible not to take up subjectivity. I was confronted with the complexities of situating myself as an "outsider" in relation to a movement comprised of people who have a history of oppression by a service system in which I have been a worker. In their attempts to deal with this, survivors demanded of me a particular kind of participation: they wanted me to be personal. From my point of view this meant disclosing pieces of myself I have been trained to keep private and separate in order to properly fulfill the roles of service provider, organizer and researcher. Taking up this challenge, I moved into a process of professional and personal deconstruction. I disempowered myself as a mental health professional; I gave over authority for a period of time to the survivors with whom I worked.

My articulation of this process establishes a "survivor frame" for this book — a feature which is supported by feminist poststructural theories. In forming their movement, consumers/survivors begin from "I," from their own story, usually in relation to the power and authority of the mental health system. I merely follow their example by amplifying the "private," "personal" and "emotional" dimensions of my project. There is a challenge here to (male-dominant) conventions concerning what can be discussed in academic settings and/or public consultations. It is not easily brought. There are those who have declared emotions academically legitimate, who have cried out for their inclusion (for example, Hochschild, 1978; Oakley, 1983; Duelli Klein, 1983; Rockhill, 1987; Jackson, 1990; Zola, 1991) but seldom are feelings actually written in. Rare exceptions include Rockhill (1987), Jackson (1990) and McKenna (1991). Like them, I struggle to express, celebrate and scrutinize feelings. It is the desire for these banished qualities which lies behind the decision to include my own (ill) body in this text. Making these inclusions does not wipe out the "public," "theoretical" and the "rational." Rather, it suggests that what we experience and present of ourselves as subjective or personal is simultaneously objective and public (Weedon, 1987; Jackson, 1990; Haug, 1992).

There is a modest but growing body of autobiographical literature expressive of feminist and postmodern thought in the fields of sociology and anthropology. Britzman (1989) points to a pro-reflexivity stream of literature within the sociology of education which encourages students to critically analyze their own biographies (for example Cully and Portuges, 1982; Nelson, 1986; Symth, 1987). Under the rubric of critical studies in masculinity, David Jackson (1991) traces the development of autobiographies from traditional male forms to life history work (feminist, gay, anti-sexist men's movement) to collective forms. (See for example Silverstein, 1977; Steinberg, 1977; Hearn, 1983; Fraser, 1984; Walkerdine, 1985; Steedman, 1986; Oakley, 1987; Grieg, 1987). Two significant feminist works which he doesn't mention are by Heilbrun (1988) and Mairs (1986; 1989). Jackson's own work incorporates feminist concerns with understanding the interaction between social forces and personal stories, and the postmodern critique of an essentialist concept of self.

DiGiacomo (1988) notes that it is postmodernism which opens up the biographical to academic scrutiny as an antidote to work which is "author-evacuated" (See Geertz, 1988: 10). She is particularly interested in social scientists who have written, as she has (1987), sociologically or anthropologically about their forays into the "kingdom of the sick" (Roth, 1963; Killian, 1975; Zola, 1982; Murphy, 1987; Frank, 1991). Zola's "socio-auto-biography" is a key piece of this literature. To these sources I would add Paget (1990), a medical sociologist specializing in medical mistakes who was herself the victim of such an error, and Orr (1990) who offers a feminist inquiry into the social and political economy of panic disorder including herself as someone so diagnosed.

There are very few feminists among the women and men who constitute the psychiatric survivor movement as I know it; I was not a feminist when I became a doctoral student. It and I became feminist together as feminist theories bridged the multitudinous gaps which existed for me between the survivor movement and academia and my life. They did this primarily by giving intellectual legitimacy to personal narrative and experiential knowledge. Poststructuralism added another dimension to this by asserting that, "There is no such thing as removing the observer from the knowledge acquisition process, since to do so would be like trying to see without eyes" (Stivers, 1993: 311). These are critical theoretical points of reference for me, and potentially, for the psychiatric survivor movement which struggles to sustain an integrative intellectual framework (Chamberlin, 1990; Dain, 1991).

Not long ago I wrote a short "history" of recent developments in the Ontario psychiatric survivor movement. Shortly after the document was released, I came home to a message on my answering machine which stated that I had broken the caller's heart by not naming him and his efforts in the text. This story points to one of the risks inherent in an autobiographical approach: the possibility of diminishing other people's voices. Naming and acknowledging Others is important, particularly in the survivor movement; there is so little public understanding or recognition of people's labors. Yet, in these pages, I choose to foreground my own voice. This is not narcissism; it is not an egocentric indulgence. I assume that knowledge is constructed.[6] Therefore, it is important to convey not just *what* the subject is but also *who* the subject is. The tales of "what" and "who" contained in these pages constitute the method by which I create a knowledge of psychiatric survivors.

Critical autobiography is vital intellectual work. It celebrates survivor voice while moving the "observer" directly into view in the knowledge construction process. The social analysis accomplished by this form is based on two assumptions: first, that it is possible to learn about the general from the particular; second, that the self is a social phenomenon (Stivers, 1993). I assume that my subjectivity is filled with the voices of other people (Lionet quoted in Stivers, 1993). Writing about myself is a way of writing about those others and about the worlds which we create/inhabit. The process uses my life, the life of one social being, to penetrate the social relations of "consumer participation." Because my subjective experience is part of the world, the story which emerges is not completely private and idiosyncratic. The issues and arguments raised are significant beyond my life and beyond the field of community mental health. They reflect changes happening in our under-standing of knowledge. They constitute an argument for how to write social science.

NOTES

1. Consumer participation is the most recent expression of deinstitutionalization, a key feature of mental health service systems in advanced capitalist nations since the 1960s. In Ontario, the policy is emerging primarily as a result of

shifting alliances between two groups. One group is comprised of psychiatric "consumers" or "survivors." They are generally understood to be "people with direct experience of significant mental health problems who have used the resources available from the mental health system" (Pape, 1988: 48). Sometimes affiliated with each other, sometimes not, these individuals have decided to participate with professionals in system development and/or reform. The other group is comprised of mental health professionals in the rehabilitation stream of the system. This is a mix of professional and paraprofessional workers, many trained in social work, nursing or occupational therapy, who staff community programs (e.g., case managers). Psychiatrists are generally not engaged in "consumer participation." With one or two notable exceptions, they are shadowy figures in this drama, powerful figures glimpsed only out of the corner of the eye. Consumer participation is played out in the cracks and holes of psychiatric hegemony. The art form practiced by the players is a kind of interstitial politics. Consequently, this book does not speak to or about psychiatrists, or about psychiatry as a structure of domination within the service system and survivor lives.

2. When I speak of the "mental health system" I am referring primarily to community services. Provincial mental health service systems in Canada are generally understood to have two major sectors: institutional and community. The institutional sector, or formal mental health care system, is understood to be "hospitals, agencies, programs, and professionals who are responsible for the provision of therapeutic treatment to people with a psychiatric diagnosis" (Pape and Church, 1987: 5). In Ontario, through the Mental Health Facilities Branch of the Ministry of Health, the government funds various facilities including ten provincial psychiatric hospitals, four specialized psychiatric hospitals and over sixty general hospital psychiatric units (Lord, 1987). The "community" sector is understood to refer to groups and agencies which deliver psychosocial services to the "mentally ill" outside of psychiatric hospitals/units/clinics (Pape and Church, 1987). In Ontario, through a Community Mental Health Branch of the Ministry of Health, the government funds more than three hundred groups and about five hundred programs which match this description.

3. Feminist poststructuralism: I don't take either of these terms or their combination as unproblematic. However, I don't want to take up how they are problematic in this particular context. I only want to give the reader some orientation to my use of this term. It is, above all, very general, stemming from a desire for " less fixed and determined ways of looking" (Lather, 1991: 39) which are at the same time rooted in an understanding of systemic disadvantage. For me there is the possibility with feminist poststructuralism of having a politics of difference which does not exclude knowledge of ordered oppression through gender, class, etc.

4. In a recent address to medical sociologists, Zola calls for a reexamination of some of the same dichotomies that I attempt to address here: "objective ver-

sus subjective; public versus private; dispassion versus affect; political neutrality versus political stances; distance versus intimacy" (1991: 8).

5. Weedon (1987) points out that the "subjective" is a term of significance within feminist theory "since the ways in which people make sense of their lives is a necessary starting point for understanding how power relations structure society" (p. 8). "Subjectivity" is also central to poststructuralist theory. My use of the term is congruent with Jackson's summary. "From these new perspectives, the poststructuralist concept of 'subjectivity' replaces the essential, authentic self.... Instead of a single, unchanging self waiting to be unburied, poststructuralist decenters the traditional self and introduces the possibility of multiple selves, much more fragmented and contradictory in make-up, being socially formed within changing conditions, relations and frameworks" (1990: 40).

6. Weedon distinguishes three types of feminism: liberal, radical and socialist. Socialist feminists understand the world as socially constructed. "Socialist feminism does not envisage a true and natural femaleness, but sees gender as socially produced and historically changing" (1987: 4). This is where I locate myself.

CHAPTER 2

Speaking

You have probably all noticed that there are a number of word battles going on in the mental health field these days. At a conference I attended recently one of the presenters billed herself as a patient/client/consumer/survivor! Many people are frustrated by this type of thing but I think it is vitally important. I believe that language is a site of struggle which is as important as the way the system is structured or the way that budgets are allocated. So we must pick our way through this carefully.

From my remarks to the Queen Street Mental Health Centre's Community Advisory Board, Toronto, February 14, 1991

Research is composed of many stories. Van Maanen notes that his monograph on writing ethnography began as "a frivolous celebration of the often informal, profane, ludicrous, and mock-heroic stories fieldworkers privately tell of their research adventures," in contrast with their public seriousness about Method (1988: xi). I was delighted when I read this. I remembered nodding in agreement as I listened to John McKnight (1986) talk about how stories are characteristic of people who are in "community." They have been an important part of my work on issues of mental health and of my relationships with psychiatric survivors.

To tell my tales, I must use words and these words are not always of my own choosing. As Britzman points out, "Using language is always a negotiation because words are slippery and elusive; they bear the capacity to assert another's intention, another meaning, another word" (1989: 10). At the very another's intention, another meaning, another word" (1989: 10). At the very least the words I use require some explanation; they themselves tell a variety of tales. Making these explicit connects me with feminist concerns about language as "a site of struggle" (Weedon, 1987: 9) and with the poststructural assertion that language is productive and constitutive rather than reflective and representative (Weedon, 1987; Lather, 1989, 1991).[1]

In the pages which follow I use the words "psychiatric survivor" and "consumer/survivor" to refer to people who are popularly thought of as mentally ill, crazy, nuts, crackers, bananas, schizy, loony and so on.... I talk about how I came to be involved with psychiatric consumers/survivors and how that involvement shifted and changed over the past decade. I use these words because, of all the choices I have available to me, they are the ones I am most comfortable with right now. This is a political decision which is intimately wound up with my long transformation from being a children's therapist in Saskatchewan to being a Toronto-based researcher/activist.

As a clinician I was familiar with labelling theory; doing intelligence testing I had to grapple with identifying children as "mentally retarded" or "developmentally delayed." A significant portion of the first document I wrote for the Canadian Mental Health Association (CMHA) was concerned with words and definitions (Church and Pakula, 1983). The insights that I had then continue to be relevant to me. Simply put, there are three broad coexisting sets of ideas which shape practice in the mental health field.[2] The first one is the pathology or medical model exemplified by the practice of psychiatry. Psychiatric theory presumes an illness stemming from organic or psychological processes internal to individuals. Psychiatric diagnoses are the primary criteria for identifying people as mentally ill. A mild challenger to the medical model is the rehabilitation model. Like the medical model it is focuses on diagnosis and treatment but begins to suggest that physical and social environments are as important as biochemistry or the unconscious in shaping people's behavior. The third set of ideas is about self-help. Self-help begins to challenge the notion of scientific expertise and to place both the definition of the problem and the response to it within the hands of the people who are labelled or diagnosed.

Particular words signal each model. Although there is tremendous variation within the field, it is possible to tell where people are located by listening to how they talk. As Bakhtin points out:

> All words have the "taste" of a profession, a genre, a tendency, a party, a particular work, a particular person, a generation, an age group, the day, the hour. Each word tastes of the context in which it has lived its socially charged life; all words and forms are populated by intentions. (1981: 293)

And so psychiatrists talk about their "patients"; practitioners of rehabilitation talk about "clients" or "consumers" of service. Terms within the self-help sector range from no labels at all to "ex-patient inmate" to "consumer" to "survivor." The movement from one model to the next implies a rearrangement of people's relationships from more to less passive and hierarchical.

Ideas:	Pathology	Rehabilitation	Self-Help
Words:	patient	client	member
	illness	disability	consumer
			ex-patient
			ex-inmate
			survivor

This formulation was my first glimmer of understanding language post-structurally, in terms of competing discourses, "competing ways of giving meaning to the world, which imply differences in the organization of social power" (Weedon, 1987: 24). However, my initial observations about language were apolitical. It wasn't until I became a doctoral student that I began to seriously probe their political implications. Then I could be explicit about the fact that the three conceptual models I had identified do not have equivalent status within the mental health field. The medical model is dominant; psychiatric terminology has entered common parlance. It defines the terms for discussion in "a variety of forms, and at a variety of levels of sophistication ... in the professional journals, in the popular and semi-popular literature of paperback books, women's magazines and columns such as Ann Landers" (Smith and David, 1975: 2). Control over symbolic representation is vested with mental health professionals. The "mentally ill" themselves have very little influence on the words and images which describe them. Verbal disempowerment is a major part of their experience.

In the current psychiatric system, the power to speak is given exclusively and unjustly to the psychiatrist. The psychiatrists-as-oppressors impose their words on the patients-as-oppressed. At the same time, the "patients" (psychiatric inmates) are robbed of their words. They have no say about what happens to them, and they are not listened to or believed. (Burstow and Weitz, 1988: 22)

For this reason, some radical ex-patients consider themselves to have been "psychiatrized."

These differences are not simply theoretical. When I worked for the CMHA arguments over words and labels were an integral part of my daily life. They were a major part of the struggle to write documents which might shape policy. I belonged to a group which attempted to supplant the organizational use of the words "psychiatric patient" and "chronically mentally ill" with a variety of other terms. We were concerned about the stigmatizing effects of labels and about reducing people to illnesses or conditions, for example by referring to someone as "a schizophrenic." Our experiments in search of more validating language were awkward and frequently not effective. They included: people labelled psychiatrically disabled; people with severe mental disabilities; people who have directly experienced the mental health system; users of mental health services; consumers of service. By the time I left the organization I was most familiar with using the term "consumer."

There are two advantages to this word. It is psychiatrically neutral and it anticipates a significant restructuring of the service system through user purchasing power. But there is by no means a consensus around "consumerism" primarily because, for some former psychiatric patients, it doesn't make as potent a political statement as the term "psychiatric survivor" (Barker and Peck, 1987).

Student: What is the difference between a consumer and a survivor?

Kathryn: There is a difference in the degree of anger and political activity communicated by the two words. "Consumer" is more neutral; "survivor" is more inflammatory. It makes professionals angry to think that people would label themselves as survivors of a system which they think is helpful. "Survivor" had an edge for awhile but it has lost it just in the last six months. I wrote a brief recently in which I used both terms: "consumer/survivor." About three weeks later after it was presented I began to hear people talking about consumers/survivors. I thought "Wait a minute!" Now I hear the term everywhere. The language in this area is so fluid. (Transcript of doctoral students' discussion, March 1991)

I began to use the term "psychiatric survivor" after I left the CMHA. I had given some thought to the argument that "consumer" carries with it a false implication of service choice and that:

There is a striking parallel between consumers of services and consumers of commodities: both are out of control of what they consume; both stand outside the determinants of the process of production; both act in response to a definition of their needs outside their conscious control; and both are passive recipients of the interaction which reproduces existing power relations. (Rose and Black, 1985: 37)

In the last few years I have spent quite a bit of time with people who call themselves "psychiatric survivors"; I have become comfortable with this term. It labels but it does so in a way which I find affirming of people's strengths, one which I can identify with personally. However, I do not use it rigidly, primarily because of my experience working with groups. I have also spent time with users of the system who were uncomfortable with the confrontational nature of "psychiatric survivor" and its implication that what is to be survived is not "mental illness" but psychiatric treatment. In practice I use the words which are preferred by the people I am with at any given time.

Written work is different. Choices must be made and, especially within academia, one's own position is expected to be paramount. My writing moves back and forth between "consumer/survivor," a term I first used in 1990 (Reville and Church), and "psychiatric survivor." I use more than one term to reflect my sensitivity to the unresolved language wars within what was originally the ex-psychiatric inmate liberation movement, and to reflect the territory in which I work as an activist/researcher. This is yet another place to start with speaking. My choice of words is not immutable; I anticipate changes in my speaking/writing practices.

NOTES

1. Britzman notes that, for Bakhtin, language "is not a neutral medium shaped by individual desire or intent, or bordered by objective meanings. Rather, it is the symbolic terrain where hegemony is fought" (1989: 10).

2. I use the word "ideas" here because that is the word I would have applied at the time I formulated this schema. Today I would use the word "discourse," thinking of it in the Foucauldian sense as not just words but also practices, "ways of knowing that simultaneously — and under specific historical conditions and in interaction with other kinds of discourse — bring into being the object of knowledge" (DiGiacomo, 1988: 113).

CHAPTER 3

Acting

> In your action is your knowing.
> Lather, *Getting Smart*

Most research is designed to respond to issues defined by established bodies of academic literature within particular disciplines. Research papers then become a conversation among academics; they are of limited relevance to other groups and the general public. In order to produce an accessible knowledge of "consumer participation," I began with action rather than academic literature. My research with and for psychiatric survivors was shaped by the incidents and activities I encountered as an activist. My route through it was determined by people other than myself, by confrontations and opportunities offered to me. George Smith captures the essence of this approach:

> The first step in the research, consequently, was not a study of the relevant sociological literature. The focus of my investigations did not arise theoretically in this way. Nor did I start by trying to construct a bird's-eye view of a regime. I never collected data using a standard protocol with the intention of making sense of it later. Nor was my access to the field organized from within a politico-administrative regime, using university affiliations or organizational structures close to hand. I did not go about arranging interviews from my office, using my professional credentials to gain entree to the field, for example. (Smith, 1990: 638)

Instead, investigative activities were driven by the political strategy of a particular group, in this case, of gay men and "the route of access was determined by the course of confrontation" (Smith, 1990: 18). Thus, in a study on policing the gay community, data came through events such as first person accounts of policing activities, meetings with defense attorneys and attending court. The second stage involved presenting briefs and making presentations to various components of the criminal justice system. The third stage involved consultations with "experts" and reading the academic literature.

The interconnected stories in this chapter "map" where I was situated throughout my research and the relationships which made it possible. The picture looks a little bit like Snakes and Ladders (Figure 1). It can be read chronologically from the top to the bottom of the page but the reader should not be taken in by this apparent order. Inside, I lived the climbing and sliding gamble of the board game. To convey this textually, I have broken the ordered, logical, unitary flow of my narrative with quotes from journals, with reflections and vignettes which point to the uncertainty and turbulence accompanying "what happened."[1] The map of my engagement expresses a central tenet of feminist poststructuralism, namely that "all knowledge is contingent on the details of its local production, is 'relative to' those practices done in those places" (Schneider, 1991: 296). I have created a knowledge of "consumer participation" from where I existed physically, from what I did, what I observed and the people I was involved with.

DOING NATIONAL ORGANIZING

In my early days with the Canadian Mental Health Association I was excited about the thought of working at a national office. I looked forward to broadening my knowledge of Canada, to discovering those pieces of it which are psychologically invisible out west. Surely here things of national importance were being done. And (for once, not like on the prairies) I could be at the heart of it. Over five years with the Association I discovered that it was very difficult to orchestrate anything of importance to the mental health world from inside CMHA National. A low budget operation, the office occupies the top floor of a small office building in the Yonge-Eglinton area of Toronto. Miles away from the national capital in Ottawa, its connection to national events and policy-makers is remote. To complicate matters further, mental health policies and legislation are a provincial not a federal responsibility.

At that time the office housed two very different types of workers. Some were permanent employees who looked after running the organization (its annual conference, employee pensions, etc.). Others were temporary employees working on program and policy development whose salaries were dependent upon contract funds gleaned from a combination of private foundations and federal government departments. The national program director

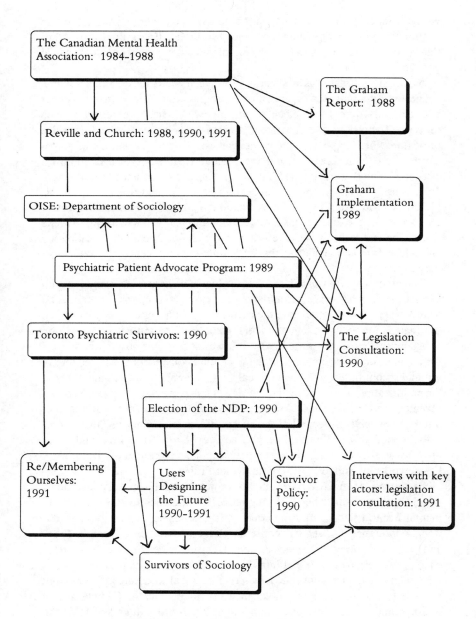

Figure 1. Mapping my own engagement.

wore the latter like armor in his quest to rejuvenate the organization through "national community development" (see Morwood, 1984). I became part of this "team"; these people shaped my initial understanding of how to do social change.

My first contract was a success. I wrote a readable document which suggested directions for organizational programming. I was given another contract, this time for a piece of writing which had previously proven difficult. The task was to generate a position paper on mental health service provision which expressed the somewhat contradictory opinions of an as-sortment of "volunteers" called the Mental Health Services Committee. These volunteers were not the kind who put the coffee on at the local drop-in. They were "players" in the mental health system from a variety of locations. I knew very little about system organization or policy but I could put forward the essence of the discussions I was listening to and I was learning to make deals. The end result was a carefully negotiated document which addressed enough individual agendas to make possible the emergence of a collective message.

The document advanced the notion that consumers of mental health services should be active participants in planning and operating the mental health system. Writing this into the policy paper, a "progressive" idea which originated not with me but with my volunteer committee, was my first exposure to "consumer participation." It was at that time strictly theoretical for me and for the organization. There were no consumers of service on my volunteer committee, none on national staff, and none sitting as members of the national board. Following the successful publication of the position paper (Trainor and Church, 1984), I was given yet another contract to pull together into one cohesive project all of the program division's work on "the chroni-cally mentally ill." Working on the advice of my committee and other program staff I coordinated the emergence and development of "Building A Framework For Support" (The Framework Project).

By the time I left CMHA in 1988 this project had published six documents which were well-distributed through CMHA branches to the community mental health sector across the country. It had hosted two national invita-tional conferences: a "search" conference on empowerment (Church, 1986) and a national policy conference designed for mental health bureaucrats from each province/territory. It had introduced some new words into the CMHA vocabulary and created some new organizational structures. Framework volunteers had given public talks in every major city in Canada and at international conferences including the 1987 World Congress of Mental Health in Cairo. Federal funds had been secured for pilot site demonstrations. This sounds like "success" and "progress" and in a sense that is the impression I wish to convey. Doing this work gave me a strong sense of helping to build something worthwhile. I might have continued in this vein had it not been for the parallel development of forces within the project and the national office which combined to move my life to other locations and ways of thinking.

The project's national search conference in 1985 transformed "consumer participation" from words on paper to flesh and blood. It brought together an amazing assortment of people whose attitudes to being at a CMHA-sponsored event ranged from delight to hostility and whose politics ranged from conservative to radical. Thus, my first serious exposure to people who were "mentally ill" was not in a clinical setting but at a policy-making exercise. The consumers/survivors who attended the conference became fundamental to the project; structures were invented to give them formal status. They became important to me personally. I kept in touch with them by telephone and periodic face-to-face meetings. I learned from them about the day-to-day circumstances of their lives and the difficulties of "participation." Running the project demanded planning and organization. By contrast, consumer/survivor lives were a continual stream of unexpected and destabilizing events: people were hospitalized or disoriented by medication/s; they lost their jobs; they lost their housing; travel was difficult; poverty sucked their energy. Many times I stood by helplessly while someone's life came unglued and he/she disappeared temporarily or permanently from view.

In the first two years of the Framework project there was quite a bit of room inside CMHA for experimenting with ideas and practices. The national program division was embryonic; the more established parts of the organization viewed its scattered initiatives with amused tolerance. This changed. The energy of the national search conference was the catalyst. The Mental Health Services Committee began to come together around its own position paper and to develop its membership. Initially confused about what might be accomplished, the committee became clear that it wanted the needs and democratic rights of the most marginalized "mentally ill" to become central (again) to CMHA.[2] Members talked about a significant increase in the number of consumers/survivors sitting on the national board; they wanted a reexamination of budgetary priorities. Then, in the spring of 1985, the chairman of the committee and I persuaded David Reville to become the group's first consumer/survivor member.

David was then the member of provincial parliament for Riverdale in Toronto. He had been a city alderman. In both roles he spoke openly about his experiences as a psychiatric patient; he was a seasoned advocate on behalf of the "mentally ill." David's membership on the Mental Health Services Committee sharpened its profile considerably within the CMHA. Gradually the implications of the project were perceived by the organization's chief decision-makers; room for development began to disappear. It was monitored more closely to see that its activities did not jeopardize other organizational activities and sources of funding. I watched this battle played out in national board meetings, in the focus and tone of national fund-raising campaigns, in communications strategies and conference programs. I experienced it most profoundly within the national office itself.

As program division projects became prominent, as more staff were hired, as more volunteers and survivors appeared on the scene, other employees felt deeply threatened. The two factions in the office split. Communication between them was difficult and frequently hostile. Going to work was like walking into an armed camp. The battle raged for more than two years ending only with the retirement of the general director. Then there was The Fall-Out. The program division came apart at the seams as battles which we had suppressed for the sake of solidarity surged to the surface. People who had been mutually supportive for years suddenly turned on each other. We were knee-deep in betrayal. In the spring of 1988, hurt and exhausted by all that had happened, I walked out without saying good-bye to my co-workers. The work of the organization had become a problem for me and I had doubts about the possibilities for organizational change. I had become committed to working on behalf of consumers/survivors but was left with burning questions about how.

> What is going on here? I am attempting to confront a tremendous loss in my life — a whole series of tangible and intangible losses and deaths.... The brokenness, the bitterness of feeling betrayed, the isolation. Now what I must face is the loss of the work which organized my day to day existence and gave my life such a strong sense of meaning. Coping with this is a large and complicated task. It touches on the root question of my whole existence. Why am I here? Having lost the vehicle by which I have worked on this question for the past five years, I feel tremendously empty. I am afraid of slipping away into meaninglessness and obscurity, spending my time worrying about how to get the wash really clean and how to lose that extra ten pounds and other adventures of minimal importance. I have no way right now of making a contribution where it really matters and very little patience for resting until I can create new channels for myself. I am afraid that I will never again do anything worthwhile, that I will sit on the edge of events and spectate as other people act. (Journal entry, May 1988)

DOING ACADEMIA

In the fall of 1989 I entered the doctoral program in sociology at the Ontario Institute for Studies in Education (OISE). After auditing a summer class on policy formation I could see that in this environment new light would be shed on the questions I had about my CMHA experience. I cannot remember whether or not I sensed that the questions and experiences themselves would be recast. I do know that I was intensely frustrated with a particular configuration of words and phrases which I heard repeated endlessly in mental health meetings and conferences. My mind had gone numb with their cadence:[3]

community caring community living supportive
community acceptance community service integration
community resource base community mental health care
system policy program planning coordination resources
illness disability needs rights psychiatric hospital clients
institutional deinstitutional service comprehensive range
continuity alternatives development network
participation advocacy framework blueprint sectors
organization agencies professionals formal informal
volunteers model self-help function/ing population
funding legislation local regional national demonstration
proposal decision-making research issues process
documentation social action social change responsibility
partnership reallocation empowerment stakeholder
implementation citizens mechanisms lobbying
representation rehabilitation consumer user involvement

I had a deep longing to speak and write differently about what I was embedded in, to phrase my concerns in words which I had not yet heard, to break down old patterns of thought, to break through into a different perception of issues.[4] I was suspended in a dysjuncture between what was and what wasn't yet with very few words to mark the place. Becoming a student of sociology introduced me to a new constellation of words/concepts which spoke/framed the world differently:

advanced capitalist societies ideologies class gender race
age social forces public policy-making state power social
crisis research economy theory crisis paradigm social
democracy socialism discourse control politics
production reproduction critical pedagogy critical theory
socially organized social organization of knowledge
ruling apparatus methodology actual practices material
conditions epistemology ontology feminism embedded in

these relations of ruling taken up by subjectivity
dysjuncture problematic social construction political
economy global economy stratification modernity
development postmodern inequality poststructuralism
liberal humanism deconstruction language inscription
semiotic structuralism discursive voice agency
ethnography demystification empowerment reflexivity
hegemony praxis positivism science location

In these words and the structures/relations they pointed to I sensed a way to escape the conceptual and political dilemmas I was trapped in as a "national organizer." Gradually I came to see that a major part of my new project was to read the first stream of words in light of the second, to re-inscribe my knowledge of community mental health practices.

There was an enormous amount of intellectual joy for me in this shift. At the same time it introduced new tensions into my life. I wanted my studies to connect with consumers/survivors. I did not want to disappear into a library for four years to emerge with a degree which was untouched by the hands and minds of the people I had become connected to at some personal cost. I wanted my research to be actively political in the sense that it expressed and contributed to consumer/survivor struggles. However, it was difficult to connect with these struggles as a student. The social relations of academia themselves mitigate against outside activities. Dehli puts it this way:

> The pressures to write, research or teach within specific forms, for example, by showing "mastery" of "the literature," are embedded in the ways university education is put together and practiced. Learning how to use difficult concepts, reciting the arguments of "great" theorists, or publishing in scholarly journals is a hard and time-consuming business. It is this kind of work rather than political activism and personal history which counts as properly academic. The more feminists adjust their work to these parameters, the more we risk being split from transformative politics within and beyond the universities. (1991: 29–30)

There were two other major difficulties. I had to challenge the "intellectual houseworker" role to which many former colleagues (mostly men) had assigned me. Simultaneously, I had to overcome the suspicions which consumers/survivors had about me arising from my work history and my status as a "professional."

Breaking with the Past

Most of the people in my life expected me to do the Ph.D. as quickly as possible and to return myself virtually unchanged (perhaps with a few new skills) to the place/s I had left. I found this impossible. My (yet again) vantage point as a student allowed me to see the mental health system and my own previous role/s in it in profoundly re/disturbing ways. In the years I spent at CMHA I came to view myself as "progressive." I was liberally anti-psychiatry and anti-institutional; I was pro-community alternatives. I had questions about my role but I managed to retain a sense of working for consumer/survivor liberation. Re/doing academia stimulated me to rethink my own relationship to the system. With no job at risk and with the encouragement of professors and other students, I could critique policies and practices which, in some cases, I had helped to establish. I began to perceive my role in inscribing consumers/survivors into non-liberatory frameworks. I began to examine how we were differently caught up together in a complex web of structural inequity the threads of which were beyond our control. I lost my sense of being one of the good guys.

Lather points out that doing deconstructive academic work "includes the development of a Foucauldian awareness of the oppressive role of ostensibly liberatory forms of discourse" (1989: 10). I was acquiring this disturbing awareness; engaging with it disrupted and reorganized many existing relationships which were both professional and personal. I began to refuse jobs which people offered to me particularly where they involved disembodied document-writing which might consolidate consumer participation as simply a new feature of the same old service system. Former colleagues, some of whom (I discovered) had elevated me to icon status were mystified by my disengagement from my customary role. I was viewed as having burned all my bridges back to a useful future role in favor of the rarified "unreal" atmosphere of academe.

Doing academia also meant losing my initial access point of involvement with consumers/survivors. The CMHA has a mandate to be involved in the mental health field. Leaving the organization I lost the formal legitimacy bestowed upon employees by that mandate as well as the levers of legitimacy with which I had mobilized resources (successfully or not) on their behalf: an office, a telephone, secretarial help, a budget, a computer, an official title, letterhead, business cards, a job description, divisional executive directors, branch offices. This posed real problems for me as an individual seeking to be an active ally of the movement and as a researcher wanting to do activist research. I had to create a new (subject) position other than "service provider" or "CMHA organizer" from which to work. I began with my strongest connection to consumer/survivors: David Reville.

I was disoriented in the summer following my departure from CMHA. I wasn't interested in finding a new job. I didn't know what to do next. So when David Reville offered me a contract to write a paper for him to present at an international "users" conference I jumped at the chance (Church and Reville, 1988). This was the beginning of an informal partnership between us. For his part, David deliberately opened up routes for me into mental health politics and the many worlds of psychiatric survivors. He developed a habit of inviting me to sit in on the places where his work as a politician became the work of a survivor activist:

> question period at Queen's Park: Social Development Committee hearings; the Collins and Callahan private member's bills; Ontario Friends of Schizo-phrenics; the Psychiatric Nurse's Interest Group; Street Health; Street City; Toronto's local Board of Health; the Maytree Foundation; the Luna Circle; canvassing in Riverdale and High Park; advocacy legislation; the Attorney General's policy advisors; Brockville Survivors in Action; Dixon Hall in Toronto; Able Enterprises in Simcoe; the PEST analysis done by the Mental Health Facilities Branch; Toronto Psychiatric Survivors.

In the course of events David gave me three critical openings. He introduced me to Pat Capponi, another psychiatric survivor leader; he secured my involvement with a project called Users Designing the Future; he hired me to do a piece of "action research" on behalf of Toronto Psychiatric Survivors (TPS). In all three cases he vouched for me with the survivors involved until I could establish (or not) my own legitimacy with them and their projects.

Do the Right Thing* Right

In the spring of 1990, the Ontario government sponsored a consultation on community mental health services legislation. A legislative committee trav-elled to regional meetings in seven cities to hear presentations. As he watched these events unfold, David Reville was concerned both about consumer/sur-vivor representation on the committee and about the submissions which psychiatric survivors across the province could make to it. He believed that unless somebody paid focused attention to adequate representation it wouldn't happen. He hired me to analyze survivor involvement in the consultation.

Over a four-week period I conducted sixty telephone interviews with key informants. I sent a formal invitation from David to any groups/individuals who needed encouragement to attend. I collected written information about the consultation from all over the province. I attended two public hearings. I organized an "exit interview" after the hearings with members of a self-help group to discuss their participation in the event and the issues which concerned them. I wrote my findings into a brief called "Do the Right Thing* Right" which was presented to the Toronto hearings of the legislative committee. The organizing I did in connection with this brief extended my survivor connections; it introduced me to bureaucrats within the Ministry of Health. It also precipitated complex emotional changes.

> I was in tears at the Kingston consultation. I couldn't take it. I had to leave the room. And these funny crazy people came out and said "It will be all right." It was too much. All the professionals sat there very tightly as I roared out in tears and the crazy people came out and said "we know." It was so amazing! The people who should be really sensitive — they have had all the advantages, right? — those people were all dried up like little peas. And the people who have every reason to be broken down, they have got their hearts ripped open. They are there. They are present. I couldn't bear it. (Excerpt from SOS transcript, October 1990)

Re/membering Ourselves

In the summer of 1989 I wrote a paper for the Ontario Psychiatric Patient Advocate Office (PPAO) on advocacy and empowerment (Church, 1991a). In it I suggested that the practice of systems advocacy by the PPAO should include a proactive expansion of its partnership with psychiatric survivors. I was asked to present my formulations to the twelve patient advocates at their annual fall case conference. I felt uncomfortable talking about empowerment and partnership without having a survivor present so I asked David Reville to do the event with me. Pat Capponi was also involved as a member of the PPAO's community advisory board. Pat managed to sit through the morning as a room full of professionals politely responded to my ideas about advocacy. As she listened she became more and more enraged at what she heard. She heard a lack of urgency. She heard a lack of confrontation. She heard people being patronizing.

Pat hijacked the afternoon agenda. She had one of her infamous 18 point lists — things which were wrong with the advocate program. It boiled down to a simple message. "You guys aren't doing your job. You aren't advocates. You are part of the problem. You are not on our side. If you haven't accomplished anything by now you should quit." Now it was the advocates' turn to be outraged. How dare she judge them? Who was she anyway? Who did she represent? What did she know about anything? I had seen similar arguments break out in CMHA meetings so the confrontation wasn't new to me. All the same I had never seen it done more definitively. (I came to think of it as The Capponi Effect.) This was my working introduction to Pat Capponi, someone David had been talking to me about for months and the person he considered to be the foremost psychiatric survivor leader in the province.

The following spring I asked David and Pat to help me create a "survivor-directed" doctoral research project. I wrote them a four-page memo describing what I wanted to do and we met to discuss it. At least I thought we would discuss it. More pressing on Pat's agenda was me as a human being and whether I had the legitimacy to undertake this project. She questioned my attitudes, my values, my feelings, my strength for such a work. I should have anticipated her approach but I was feeling too well protected by my existing associations with consumers/survivors. Pat's words quickly stripped that away. It was my turn to feel hurt, insulted and outraged.

> She doesn't know if I can feel the pain these people feel. I am too cool and smooth for her.... She wants to see my pain and my passion so that she can trust me and I being intensely private (prairie roots et al.) am congenitally disposed to hiding all that. I won't trot it out on anyone's command — not even those who have a claim on it. But my whole body aches with what I feel.... I did NOTHING for the rest of that Monday except absorb physically what Pat had said. I admit that I blocked some of it, repressed it. Even trying to write it here is an effort.... What can this lesbian broad in the black hat and fake cowboy clothes possibly know about the thousands of painful acts of personal development that have brought me to this project??!! (Journal entry, March 1990)

Instead of engaging with my project, Pat suggested a different course of action. I needed to get myself "roughed up" on the front line, see what the lives of the people were really like. She suggested I go down and see how things were at Parkdale Activity and Recreation Centre (PARC), a drop-in centre on Queen Street West where she had worked for several years. I agreed. Pat met me at PARC, introduced me to the regulars, showed me around the building. I spent the afternoon chopping onions for the evening meal and trying to talk with people whose worlds were a mystery to me. Pat was at home, confident and competent; I was an outsider, uncertain and awkward.

As I contemplated the differences between us, circumstances shifted our relationship. The legislation committee announced its public hearings and I began to track its consumer participation. Pat was a member of the committee and as such had first hand experience of the organizing I was able to do. We were participants on the same side of the process and therefore had something to discuss which was held in common. That winter Pat became part of the advisory committee for a project called "Users Designing the Future." After the meetings a group of us would go out to talk about what was happening with psychiatric survivors, with mental health and with our lives generally. Over drinks in smoky bars she became for me not just a psychiatric survivor, but Pat. I became not just a professional, but Kathryn.

The August following the public hearings Pat offered me a contract to write about a program she was developing for psychiatric survivor leadership facilitation. She was inundated with requests from people wanting to learn about what she was doing but she had little written down to offer them. I had the wit to recognize that Pat was offering me on her terms what I had come to her for in the first place: a "survivor-directed" project. I took the contract, although not without reservations. I thought the work should be done by a survivor. By contrast, Pat believed that, in a bureaucratic climate which is supportive of consumer/survivor participation, many service providers will be drawn into the process and their attitude towards this venture is crucial. She thought the document required a professional who could talk across the gap between providers and consumers. She saw me as that person.

It took a year to write the document that Pat envisioned. Called "Re/Membering Ourselves" (Church and Capponi, 1991), it was constructed from material collected and/or developed by Pat for her program and from two long conversations between us in which she talked about her experiences with the program since it began in 1989. My task was to understand what she wanted to communicate, to present it in an organized way and to reflect on it from my own experience. My first draft contained the bones of the final version, but it wasn't nearly clear enough. I was in the middle of processing what I was learning from Pat, from David Reville, from Users Designing the Future, from the joys and terrors of doing a Ph.D., Pat understood this. She waited five months for the final draft to emerge. More than a thousand copies have since been distributed across Ontario and other parts of Canada.

Users Designing the Future

In the same spring as the legislation consultation, a small group of consumers/survivors received a federal grant for a project called "Users Designing the Future: A Blueprint for Mental Health in the '90s" (UDTF). David Reville took a contract to act as their facilitator. At his request I became the group's volunteer research resource. UDTF's assignment was to develop a community mental health plan from a consumer/survivor perspective. David and I worked with the group for a year. At the end of that time we had not created the plan which the group's proposal called for. Instead we had worked hard on group process and we had helped UDTF host a forum on work/jobs for a government committee looking into vocational program-ming in psychiatric hospitals.

My position with UDTF was awkward from start to finish. One explicitly stated rule guided my participation: I was to provide advice and support only on request. This was an expression of survivor politics; it was to safeguard the project from being taken over by yet another domineering professional. The strategy worked. I spent the entire project trying to figure out how to be useful to a group of people who had no experience with "research" from the position of being able to command it. I sat silently through most of the meetings, self-consciously wearing the legitimacy which David had lent to me. The goodwill of the group was undeniable but I consistently found no way to contribute my skills to their meetings. Instead, I acted as a resource to David. He and I talked frequently about what the current issues were with UDTF and how to proceed. We worked out options before taking them to the group, and over time, an analysis of the process which remained separate from it (Church and Reville, 1991).

> **Reflection**: I had a very strong sense of separation from UDTF because of the words and analytic concepts I have been trained to use. I also felt sepa-rated by the material circumstances of my life which, although not lavish, make it unnecessary for me to learn many of the survival skills which group members possess (where to buy things cheap, how to live on Family Bene-fits Allowance, which programs to use and which to avoid, for example). In contrast, the sources and evidences of my privilege (my clothing, my living situation, my schooling, my work history, my sense of the future) were a barrier which was only partially overcome within the group and then primar-ily at a personal level.

My role as mysterious but agreeable outsider remained unchanged until the forum on work raised the issue of "data collection." We taped the discussion and I worked with the transcript to identify central themes. Group members discussed these and suggested minor modifications. I was happy to be active and useful but was troubled by the fact that I conducted the analysis separately from the group. Consequently, there was no transfer of skills to members.

Interviews: The Legislative Consultation

In the winter of 1991 I turned my attention once again to the government consultation on community mental health services legislation. My initial investigation had taken only the consumer/survivor viewpoint. Now I had new questions. How was the public consultation organized? What were the practices within the mental health bureaucracy which established consumer participation as a feature of that event? To get answers to these questions I interviewed 21 key people who organized, developed and/or participated in the process. Eleven of them were government bureaucrats at different levels; three of them were government appointees; seven were consumers/survivors.

Foucault's (1981) discussion of method suggests that in documenting social practices the researcher should attend to what is said, what is done, the rules imposed, the reasons given for those rules, plans formally documented and rules/plans taken for granted. I used this as the general framework for my interviews. My questions focused specifically on five key areas, namely:

- establishing the terms of reference and membership for the legislation committee;
- drafting a discussion document for the public hearings;
- committee attendance at a consumer/survivor "sensitization session;"
- organizing the public hearings; and
- writing the final report

The interviews took place from February to April 1991. Some were done face-to-face; others by telephone. They varied in length from thirty to ninety minutes. They took place in restaurants, bars, government offices and people's homes. All interviews were taped and transcribed.

Student: Are you discovering new things by doing the interviews?

Kathryn: Yes, on a couple of levels. There is what people say and there are the different environments in which the interviews take place. This week I went to a suite of offices in the Hepburn Block where I had this very crisp, polished interview with a fairly high level bureaucrat. The next day I drove out to see a psychiatric survivor who lives in a sparsely furnished supported housing unit. She is quite poor and disabled at this point. The connection between where people are and what they are telling you is very powerful. And then there are bits and pieces of information which people tell you. People know an incredible amount and they say it. Some of it anyway. (Transcript of doctoral students' discussion, March 1991)

The interviews must be understood within the context of the September 1990 election of the first New Democratic Party government in Ontario's history. This event and the subsequent entrance of a new set of political actors sent shock waves through the mental health bureaucracy. Of particular relevance to my research was the fact that David Reville became Special Advisor to the Premier; the issues which he had raised as opposition health critic and as a vocal psychiatric survivor suddenly took on new potency. My association with him had a significant impact on the ways in which interviewees communicated with me (The Reville Factor). The subject/object dichotomy within my work became blurry; I was embedded as a subject in the "object" of my research.

> **Student:** You are actually involved in the micro-politics which you are studying. This is going to shape your understanding. How aware are you of how your position affects what you are seeing, what people are telling you?
>
> **Kathryn:** My success in setting up some of these interviews at all has to do with the fact that I am somewhat politically sensitive right now for some people. When they are talking to me I know that they are not talking just to me. They don't really know me. They know the national policy work that I did; they know my engagement with certain other people and what that network has been doing. They have a certain thing they want to communicate to me about all of that. It has been a piece of work for me in the interviews to demonstrate to people that I am interested not just in consumer participation but in any number of different things that they have to say. (Transcript of doctoral students' discussion, March 1991)

Survivors of Sociology

By the summer of 1990 I was on the verge of an emotional and physical collapse which was/is intimately bound up with my engagement with psychiatric survivors in research and activism. I had many responses to this "breakdown" but one of the most useful was a form of self-help. I phoned four women, casual acquaintances from classes at OISE, with whom I felt an affinity: Jane Haddad, Michelynn Lafleche, Kate McKenna and Sharon Rosenberg. I described how I was feeling and what I thought it was linked to. I asked for their help. They understood and responded. We began to meet over dinner in each others' homes initially for support in doing work within OISE. I framed my own need in terms of personal survival; we called ourselves the Survivors of Sociology (SOS).[5] My initial response to this was a burst of feeling.

> My first discovery with the risk I took in disclosing my pain is that I am not alone. Each of these women has a tremendous burden to carry — some legacy of pain — which intersects with her work. Each struggles in this

environment. Feeling this in them has saved me. (Journal entry, November 1990)

As the group developed we discovered the desire to engage with each others' research; we broadened our involvement to biweekly discussions which were taped and transcribed by members. SOS required me to ask new questions about my research. Most notably, they pointed out to me that I told many stories about my activities in the world of mental health for the entertainment of the group, but deleted them from my academic writing. This compartmentalization of my involvement into private/public and formal/informal pieces was challenged at a level which was not always easy for me to absorb.

> Met with the Survivors of Sociology this morning. It is quite clear to me that our conversations — our attempts to decompartmentalize with each other — have both changed my work and catalyzed this current explosion of emotion. This is "good" — this is what I want — but it is terribly difficult/uncomfortable.... The Survivors want to see me open up more. (Journal entry, November 1990)

> Sitting at Hart House. Depressed. I just made a presentation to SOS based on an abstract developed for next week. They are supportive but found it too directed toward old models of positivistic science and not sufficiently expressive of the richness of my own descriptions of my work. (Journal entry, February 1991).

SOS urged me to describe the subjective dimensions of my work by writing in my responses to events, people and confrontations alongside my more objective findings. "Are you journaling that?" they would ask, and "Where are the bodies in this?" Encouraged by each other we all struggled to bring more of ourselves to our writing and our research.

> What has emerged somewhat unexpectedly, through our commitment to these processes is a mutual exploration of the social/discursive practices of doing academic work. In our feelings, our interactions and the responses of other people to our project we have encountered some of the unwritten rules and invisible boundaries of institutional education. Attempting to bridge the "normal" compartmentalization of our lives has forced us to confront ways in which we live out false separations of ourselves as learners. We have struggled with these separations around a number of issues: disclosure/confidentiality/trust; race and racism; personal and institutional "monogamy"; private and public; individual and collective. Gradually we have realized that they are all articulated to practices of inclusion/exclusion within education. (From an SOS abstract for a presentation to Canadian Women's Studies conference, 1991)

Kate began to talk publicly during this time about being a psychiatric survivor; our conversations about how we know this experience differently shifted and changed both of us. The mutual learning which occurred within SOS that winter permeated my project. I was deeply engaged in a complex three-way conversation involving them, professors within the sociology department, and psychiatric survivors in the "real" world. The research was mine but it passed repeatedly through the bodies/minds of Sharon, Kate, Michelynn and Jane. Without their engagement with me in ways which crossed the invisible boundaries of academia I would have lived, understood and written my knowledge of "consumer participation" very differently.

NOTES

1. Breaking the logical flow of the text has its roots in poststructuralism and feminist poststructuralism (Foucault, 1972; Weedon, 1987) and the theory of the subject (e.g., Henriques et al., 1984; P. Smith, 1988).

2. The CMHA was formed in the early 1900s as the National Committee for Mental Hygiene. The early work of the Association was focused on reforming provincial psychiatric asylums in order to introduce more modern, scientific mental health care. With "new and innovative" ideas about mental health spawned during the Second World War II, the Association's concerns shifted to encompass the mental health of Canadians in general (see Griffin, 1989; Gold, 1988). CMHA now has a very general mandate which identifies its concern for the promotion of mental health and the prevention and treatment of mental illness. Issues related to the well-being of Canadians are encompassed within this mandate. For that reason, a wide variety of concerns absorb the energies of the association; the agenda keeps changing. In 1987 the national conference program theme was "Deinstitutionalization: Empowerment or Abandonment?" The focus was on the most seriously disabled users of mental health services. By contrast, the 1988 program was build around the theme "Mental Fitness: Ours to Share." It was designed for the average Canadian; the focus was on personal growth and mental health promotion (Church and Reville 1988). The Framework Project was positioned on the side of traditional organizational concerns with the "mentally ill." It's intent, however, was to transform that side rather than to continue the work of the organization's founding (medical) "fathers."

3. I would not have broken form like this, simply pouring words out in columns, had it not been that while I was writing this section I was also reading Kate McKenna's Master's thesis (1991). I am indebted to her for the bold example she set.

4. My experience here is similar to Ellsworth's breaking out of critical pedagogy. "As I began to live out and interpret the consequences of how discourses of "critical reflection," "empowerment," "student voice," and "dialogue" had influenced my conceptualization of the goals of the course and my ability to make sense of my experiences in the class, I found myself struggling against (struggling to unlearn) key assumptions and assertions of current literature on critical pedagogy, and straining to recognize, name and come to grips with crucial issues of classroom practice that critical pedagogy cannot or will not address" (1989: 303).

5. For the sake of eliminating some clumsiness from the writing and at the substantial risk of making us seem homogeneous, I will refer to the group as SOS.

CHAPTER 4

Knowing

> Wisdom is a living stream not an icon to be
> preserved in a museum.
>
> Thich Nhat Hahn, *The Sun My Heart*

In recent years the creation of academic knowledge has become problematic, particularly in the social sciences. Positivism with its linear, singular view of the truth is waning; other approaches are increasingly influential. I was trained to analyze the world as a complex array of social relations characterized by structural inequality. I have become responsive to feminism/s and poststructuralism/s where they enliven my existing commitment to all kinds of liberatory practices (Weedon, 1989; Lather, 1989; Lather, 1991). I particularly like the feminist/poststructural emphasis on "location, embodiment, and partial perspective" (Lather, 1989: 16). It sensitizes me to the fact that, from where I was situated in the various locations on my map, some people, issues and forces are visible while others are obscured. In this chapter I trace the evolution of my particular knowledge of consumers/survivors.

KNOWLEDGE IN PRACTICE

When I first started to work with the "mentally ill" I didn't think consciously about knowledge, but I can reclaim my attitude towards it by remembering how I thought about writing for the CMHA. I was very concerned about being accurate and comprehensive in reading and summarizing relevant literature. I believed in "facts" as things which had to be ferreted out of articles, books and libraries. My job was to gather them together in one spot and systematize them for organized consumption. I was very conscious that the way in which I did this would influence what people in the organization

35

did — a weighty responsibility. Perhaps as a result, I found it almost impossible to choose between competing sets of "facts." I usually handled this by bringing forward several ways of thinking about an issue as equally weighted and worthy of consideration. I thought that choosing and writing within a particular framework constituted "bias."

As my work within the CMHA deepened, my understanding of knowledge became more explicitly value based. I began to understand that all knowledge serves certain purposes. It became a weighted and contested commodity; one had to choose where to stand in relation to it.[1] I learned to evaluate both people and ideas on the basis of how they affected the lives of consumers/survivors. So, for example, I observed that while the medical model looks for root causes and seeks a cure, the rehabilitation model looks at effects and seeks successful adjustment to disability. The medical model is concerned with biochemical or psychological processes while the rehabilitation model is concerned with functioning and must, therefore, give some consideration to the environments in which activity is taking place. The medical model leaves little room for patient participation, while the rehabilitation model sees the client as a collaborative partner. Practitioners of the medical model are invested in biochemical research as the best long-term strategy for conquering mental illness; rehabilitationists generate programs and services geared to the more immediate task of maintaining individuals outside of the psychiatric hospital.

My own values as a mental health practitioner were conditioned by the consumers/survivors who preferred self-help. The self-help sector is not a major "player" in the mental health "game" being poorly organized, the least-funded and therefore the least powerful. Self-help groups form for reasons specific to the members themselves ranging from mutual support to advocacy. Those involved are concerned with their own experience — not to adjust or change it but to communicate and validate it as a legitimate part of their lives. As a side-effect, their time together may be therapeutic or rehabilitative, but it is just as likely to be social and/or political. Self-help allows consumers/survivors themselves to look outward and identify the changes they feel should be made to their world, rather than having their needs and remedies prescribed by someone else. The model depends upon the collective initiative and participation of people who have experienced problems.

While I publicly advocated for self-help, the model posed problems for me as a professional. Active involvement of consumers/survivors in decision-making means both a decrease and a qualitative change in the professional involvement which is deemed necessary. Members of most self-help groups have an ambivalent relationship with professionals and generally exclude them from participation (Lord, 1984). As a first step in resolving this contradiction I became interested in creating "knowledge for" consumers/survivors. I thought of consumers/survivors as having different knowledge needs than those of families or professionals or mental health bureaucrats. The "facts" they required had to do with system survival: which psychiatrists and medications to avoid, where to find housing and food, how to start a self-help group, community relations, using the media, fund-raising, record-keeping, decision-making and leadership. I had not yet looked deeply at redefining knowledge itself, or at problematizing the relationship of knower to known. I was troubled by the boring, rote-like quality of my own knowledge and by "distortions" of knowledge which I saw around me. For example, I did a certain amount of public speaking in Canada about key concepts from the Framework Project and their application. I used to meet people who would say "Oh, yes we are implementing the Framework model" and proceed to describe a program which horrified me in the distance it represented from the model's intent. I thought that difficulties such as these and my own struggle to think "freshly" stemmed from not having learned the "right" knowledge yet, namely those ideas and methods which would ensure liberatory outcomes in terms of democratic rights, equality and justice.[2]

THINKING ACADEMIA

I thought perhaps doing a Ph.D. would "fix" my knowledge problems. The early indications were good. I entered the program after auditing a class on policy-making in education. The issues we discussed there were my issues framed in different terms; I felt personally validated for the experience I brought to class. And so I connected with the Department of Sociology. I thought that I had found a place where I could recover myself and make sense of my practitioner dilemmas. A tremendous hopefulness was unleashed in me with the move back to academia. The first paper I wrote that Fall marks the reemergence of Theory As Knowledge in my life and the beginning of a conscious struggle with it. My embracings of/resistances to theory continue even into this writing. Indeed they give form to what I have to say.

In those days, which now seem innocent, I wrote about my search for intellectual roots:

> I am still searching for an intellectual tradition which I can call home. I only recently realized that my ongoing experience of contradictory viewpoints reflects the ambiguities of intermediate class status. My family valued consensus. Conflict was present but never made explicit. I see people as purposeful actors who do not always accomplish what they set out to do. Some

of the limitations are personal, but there are also external forces which exert
a power influence. My world is co-constituted. The historical materialist
analysis of class, labor and capital has intellectual but little emotional meaning for me. I consider my opaqueness in this area to be significant —
something to be further investigated. I value a worldview grounded in real
life experience, although I have questions about how that becomes empirical
rather than a subjective process.

These words were prescient. In the next two years I would discover my desire
to do academic work which is both intellectual and emotional, empirical and
subjective.

Initially, the intellectual was dominant; to think was to know. I was
encouraged to begin with theory, to take a theoretical position based on
reading from which to build my work. I basked in the renewed exposure to
ideas but felt resistant to demands that I choose one particular framework.
My instincts were to come to theory from practice.

> I continue to struggle with the relationship between theory and practice. I
> brought a tremendous amount of practice knowledge into OISE with me; I
> have encountered much theory. But how do these two realities come to-
> gether? Which comes first? I am attempting to understand my experience
> theoretically. But I often feel that there is some distortion of reality at work
> here. (Memo to SOS, October 1990)

I became engaged in a tremendous amount of "doing" partly as a way of
working out this confusion. This strategy also gave me some room to
negotiate how I felt in general about becoming an "intellectual."

My struggle with theory was/is embedded in complex feelings I have
about myself and my personal history: the pragmatism of my Alberta roots,
the anti-intellectualism of my parents and the fundamentalist religion burned
into the core of my upbringing. I too have parents who are "wary, ambivalent,
mistrusting of my intellectual aspirations even as they have been caring and
supportive" (hooks, 1989: 53). And I felt answerable to consumers/survivors
for this new training. I experienced and reexperienced the fact that, while
exposure to theory was "shifting my frame," as SOS termed it, the same
could not be said for other practitioners — at least not to the same degree.
This posed a real dilemma for me: every step I took to rethink "consumer
participation" separated me further from the people I needed to work with in
order to enact a broader vision of "consumer participation."

> I have to raise a question here. If we "shift the frame" then how do we
> continue to make connections with people who haven't? We sit here, inside
> OISE, and learn to think quite differently. Nobody else is doing this. They
> are all out there thinking things the way they thought them before. What are

we going to do?... What do I do as a practitioner going into a world in which a problem is thought psychiatrically and I think it sociologically? This is becoming a sharper and sharper problem for me as OISE shifts my frame. You can call this "But Can I Get A Job?" (From SOS transcript, November 1990)

As I engaged with sociological theory, particularly with feminist poststructuralism, I was concerned about the realistic possibilities of getting a job in the mental health field. I could see that taking it seriously, allowing it to reshape my practice, would make me unfit for or unwilling to occupy the roles which are available to workers in the system. As Gusfield points out:

> A sociology that makes no pretense to instruct or lead the public, that provides no scientific rationale for the authority of its practitioners, is neither likely to be sought after by a State and its agencies nor by political critics. (quoted in Schneider, 1991: 308)

Where, then, would I locate myself? Beyond self-interest, I was concerned that this rethinking would separate me from the possibilities of connecting with other people to make changes from inside the system. This remains an active dilemma.

Political Economy

Political economy illuminated some of the sources of my frustration with my work at CMHA. As an employee of that organization I did not have (was not expected to have) an analysis of the economic context in which consumers/survivors lived out their lives; my understanding of structural inequities was weak or suppressed. I began to think mental health issues differently by reframing them in the light of political economic theories. The literature on the political economy of health suggests that our understanding about health is dominated by a scientistic paradigm which emphasizes individual biology and pathology, positivistic medical knowledge and a definition of health as the ability to function — in particular the ability to work. By contrast, the political economy of health locates both health status and health care within the prevailing social/economic context. Its focus is on social production; it assumes that the meaning of health is socially derived and our responses to it are socially produced (Kelman 1975; Doyal 1979; Waitzkin 1983; Elling 1986).

Student: Have you seen "Beautiful Dreamers" about Walt Whitman at the London Psychiatric Hospital?

Kathryn: I make a habit of never going to movies about mental illness. It isn't that I don't believe in mental illness, merely that I have set aside the debate about what it is. There are still groups of people meeting to talk about what mental illness is but this is an intellectual debate that I don't want to do anymore. I can't see a way out of it. My way is to try and figure out what the debate is sitting in. I am not so much interested in mental illness as in what happens when we decide to talk about it the way we do. (Transcript of doctoral students' discussion, March 1991)

Political economy drew me into schematizing socially produced responses to "mental illness" in terms of labor and the material resources allocated. I expanded my original formulation of mental health discourse to indicate how each of the three active models can be distinguished by the type and cost of labor involved. The medical model is characterized by professional, specialized, entrepreneurial or unionized, high-cost labor in the form primarily of psychiatrists, psychologists and nurses. Rehabilitation is practiced by many para-professional workers; they tend to be non-unionized and lower-cost. As the name suggests, self-help is basically voluntary. Its informal networks operate at virtually no cost; training is not formal. Funding for the system varies by model; it remains divided with about 95% allocated to institutions and 2–4% allocated to community agencies (Pape and Church, 1987). The operation of small groups of people is virtually unfunded (see Figure 2.)

Political economy also sensitized me to the ideological dimensions of "mental illness." I suddenly realized that the knowledge models depicted by my map of the mental health terrain were almost completely subsumed by the liberal ideology which more broadly characterizes advanced capitalist societies. My map revealed significant differences between the models but obscured their similarities. Rehabilitation does not undermine the process of segmenting people into useful/not useful pieces and turning them into sites for enquiry. With the medical model it shares a common focus on individuals as problematic; it views personal improvement by individuals as the prime measure of success. Both share a clinical orientation in which there is enormous concern with the patient–client relationship. Most significantly, both require professional experts and rely on science and technology while they are silent on issues of material exploitation and community. The adherence of these two dominant models to the tenets of liberalism explains their dominance and their entrenchment together as a treatment system operating like any other business in a capitalist economy.

Mapping the mental health terrain made starkly clear the origins of my dilemmas as a mental health policy-maker. I was aligned with consum-

Ideas:	Pathology	Rehabilitation	Self-help
Words:	patient	client	member
	illness	disability	consumer
			ex-patient
			ex-inmate
			survivor
Labor:	professional	para-professional	informal networks
	specialized		
	unionized	non-unionized	
	high cost	lower cost	no cost
	....	....	....
	psychiatrists	social workers	family
	psychologists	nurses etc. acting as	friends
	social workers	"front-line staff"	donut shop staff
	nurses	(e.g., case managers)	consumers/survivors
Funding:	government	government and/or	unfunded
	block grants	voluntary orgs.	
		charities	
	95%	2–4%	1%

Figure 2. Mapping the mental health terrain.

ers/survivors and self-help but my work emanated from more established sectors. Even my most progressive notions were hedged around by liberal ideology. Doing my own research within OISE was an opportunity to break this pattern. I went into the experience with a preference for an applied approach and methods which are qualitative rather than quantitative. I felt they could more adequately capture the realities of consumer/survivor experience. I was very much aware that consumers/survivors often reject research because they feel so alienated from both the process and the results. Research endeavors in the past have suffered from both blatant and subtle effects of power inequalities between subjects and researchers. The most pervasive is the subtle injustice which results from the objectification of the human "subjects" under study: "subjects" do not shape the questions being asked, the issues considered relevant or the methods of investigation. In place of "knowledge for" I had come to favor participatory methods which would create "knowledge with" consumers/survivors. I envisioned one further step.

> I would argue that, although it is an excellent start, it is not sufficient just to put more sensitive research tools from the existing scientific paradigm into the hands of more sensitive professionals trained in that same paradigm.... I would like to see the growth of research activity which is not the preserve of a professional elite, which is "research of" rather than "research with or for." To do so we must begin to identify ways in which nonexpert users of services are empowered to be their own understanders by undertaking research initiatives for their own purposes. This would generate a body of "decolonized knowledge" (Benston, 1987). The professional role then becomes more clearly one of observer, catalyst, communicator and mobilizer of resources or some other currently unthought of role. (From my presentation to an in-service at The Clarke Institute of Psychiatry, Toronto, February 1989)

Political economy layered another agenda onto my original thoughts about research. It suggested that the goal of research pertaining to consumers/survivors is to make explicit the forces and agents outside of immediate comprehension which shape their experience personally and in terms of policy. Research should attend to the production and reproduction of particular structures and social relations which construct power and the consenting to power. It should bring to life the interplay of progressive and constraining forces which shape consumer/survivor lives and agendas.[3] Socioeconomic forces. State involvement. A network of power operations. General conditions. Worldviews. Delineating. Critical analysis. Characterizing. Contextualizing. These words and processes entered my analysis.

Feminism

When I entered the doctoral program at OISE I was 33 years old. I had been married for 12 years. I had/have no children as a matter of (difficult, contested) personal choice. Are you married? Do you have any children? From somewhere inside me a voice keeps asking these questions. Being a child-free married woman doing a Ph.D. in Toronto separates me from the woman I was supposed to be and from all but a handful of the women I grew up with in Lacombe, Alberta. Most of them remain rooted to families and farms within a 100 mile radius of that little town. Accomplishing this separation and mourning it is one of the major works/themes of my life. Lacombe is a farming community which also relies for its economic existence on the oil and gas industries. It is full of blue sky, evergreens and men in pickup trucks. I was the only girl in a family of four children. I grew up thinking like Annie Oakley: "anything you can do I can do better." I rarely wore a dress to school. I excelled in sports. I felt alienated from my mother. At 17 I was openly a feminist. I didn't marry the dairy farmer's son. I went off to Calgary (The City) instead. When I did marry in 1975, only two years out of Baptist Bible school, I kept my name.

And then for a long time I wasn't a feminist. I don't know what happened. Perhaps this silencing had to do with trying to be a wife. Perhaps it was an attempt to forge or retain some connection with my mother. Perhaps it was "just" the struggle to do my own life. Whatever it was I became uncomfortable with the word; it lost its meaning for me. So I did not take up with consumers/survivors as a feminist. I did not look to connect with feminist theory within OISE. In fact I avoided it. I selected a male supervisor out of respect for his scholarship but also because I knew that I was entering into an authoritative process. I understood how to do male authority; female authority was out of my experience. For similar reasons I felt comfortable with "masculine" conceptual frameworks, with the certainty which came with ordering, categorizing, schematizing and systematizing inherent in something like political economy.

My "breakdown" shattered this. To think was not enough as I came apart physically and emotionally; it was also necessary to feel. To feel is also to know. My struggles with feeling reactivated my feminism and made it an active issue in my work for the first time.

> My ability to engage with feminist theory is a recent acquisition. This is another issue inside the research — the issue of professional training. I was trained in a male intellectual tradition, a male way of thinking and male social relations too. The shift out of that for me as a person has only happened in the past few years. (Transcript of doctoral students' discussion, March 1991)

Questions of process and knowing in the body were not addressed by the theories I was already engaged with. They were addressed for me through feminist methodology and theory which I encountered in a meaningful way not through reading but through the Survivors of Sociology. These four women embodied feminist theory for me; I acquired it from them almost by osmosis.

When I looked at the work done by members of SOS I was startled. They were reading books, using words and attempting projects which I was unfamiliar with and challenged by. I remember Kate's paper "Learning to Talk About It: The Politics of Re/membering" (April 1990). It was very revealing of her life, tapping painful memories which became the source of her theoretical reflections. I was very drawn to her work as a story which spoke to my own questions about living as a feeling person but I had real reservations about it as academic writing. And I was startled to encounter these reservations. Where did they come from? Why was I not conscious I had them?

> **Kathryn:** This is exactly what we have been talking about this morning: drawing questions and insights and understandings not out of the literature but out of yourself and your memories. This is not considered legitimate.

> **Kate:** I think my work is going to raise questions about knowledge. What I am trying to explore is how the boundaries around knowledge are contained or constructed.

> **Kathryn:** Well, I told you that I think your paper is really beautifully written. But, in a sense, I feel that, in terms of style, I am reading journalism. Then I realize that I am making judgements about what I will recognize as academic work; your work seems to need another word. I have that distinction inside myself. I have to ask myself questions about what I am leaving out. Why can't I get that quality into my work? (Excerpt from SOS transcript, November 1990.)[4]

Why couldn't I get feeling into my work? I had been encouraged to situate myself, to identify my vantage points and alignments. But this was not the same as revealing myself personally within the work, making the connections between my private pains/joys and the project I was constructing. I wasn't in the work as a subject. That kind of writing I kept to a small circle of friends. There was a piece called "I Went To the Doctor" which had a small but interested following (Church, 1991b). It was about my experience having a breast lump investigated. I gave a copy to Pat Capponi; she pressed me to publish it and encouraged me to always write with "that voice" — the voice that up until that time, I had allowed to live only in my journal.

Troubled by this compartmentalization I probed the ways in which my academic project was regulated:

> by language, by scholarly standards, by thesis requirements, the thesis supervisors they can or cannot find, the ways they must frame and/or alter their work to get it through, the skills and attitudes that must be acquired, the hoops that must be jumped, the things that must be left out. (McKenna, 1990: 2)

I discovered that I was leaving out a tremendous amount of what I was doing and feeling as not data, not legitimate, not academic. The challenge presented by the group and supported by feminist theory was to get it back — to get the bodies, including my own, into my writing. I came to share Michelynn's desire to "incorporate my voice into my written words and challenge the confines of traditional modes of writing on public policy development" (Lafleche, 1991). What this meant generally was becoming comfortable with work which was much less ordered, more chaotic, more passionate than I had previously produced. Work which was full of messy emotions. Angry work. I found legitimacy for this in the writings of bell hooks and Audre Lorde, for example, but it also felt important in terms of consumer/survivor issues. It resonated with those places in me which were connected with consumer/survivor lives.

Survivors of Sociology introduced me to the deconstruction of order in academic work. I remember Sharon's paper "Voices of a Struggling Subject" (December 1990). Most of it was written in three columns, in fits and starts, with breaks and repetitions and different typefaces in an experiment with form that is "evocative of the multiplicities and contradictions that (at best) are not easily rendered in the linear, hierarchial form that is 'typical' of academic writing" (p. 1). She talked about how it was not neat, tidy and complete but an attempt to be honest with the processes of coming into knowing. The risks she took with that paper, and the risks that Kate took breaking form with the writing of her master's thesis affected me profoundly, influenced me profoundly. They spoke to the pieces of my own project which wouldn't fit into academia, wouldn't be rational and orderly. They spoke to the pieces of my life which in their messiness and complexity initially connected me to survivors like Pat and David.

> I am struggling right now to "take up" feminist methodology. It has some resonance with ways in which I see the world and with things I care about. As usual, I end up attempting to integrate the different approaches. So I am thinking about: consumer participation as social regulation which is lived in the body rather than imposed from the outside; how to talk about the motivations and contradictions of the policy-maker's position, the pain and the conceptual baggage of that work; how to connect my micro level observations with the macro forces in a way which isn't so abstract that the research loses the rich texture of physical bodies and flies off into the head world; how to maintain the vitality of what I observed while connecting it to extra-local processes; how to keep my social passion for this alive while I analyze it. (Memo to David Livingstone, my supervisor, October 1990)

In all of this I was attempting to break through to a psychiatric survivor frame for my project.

BREAKING THEORETICAL "MONOGAMIES"

> But it is inevitable that they will keep changing the doors on you,
> he said, because that is what they are for; and the thing is to get
> used to it and not let it unsettle the mind. But that would mean
> not jumping and you can't. Nobody can not jump. There will be
> no not jumping. Among rats, perhaps, but among people never.
>
> E.B. White, *The Door*

Amongst ourselves, Survivors of Sociology talked about our struggles with
various "monogamies" in our lives, the demands for and resistances to
exclusiveness which we felt (and extracted) from friends, lovers, partners,
colleagues of both sexes, from sociology as a discipline and OISE as an
institute of higher education. Within academia I was unable to be theoretically monogamous. I was seduced by many conceptual frameworks, strained
by conflicting loyalties: slipping back to the comfort of liberal humanism,
trying to be faithful to political economy, sneaking out to meet feminism,
flirting with poststructuralism.

Kathryn: I know what I am going to be asked at the doctoral students'
meeting. They are going to ask about theory. Where do I locate
myself theoretically? And I am going to go PHHT!! I don't know.
Sort of here. Sort of there. Sort of somewhere else.

Sharon: I think that is exactly where you locate yourself. This isn't wrong.
This is one of the things that has to shift. The notion that there is
one meta-theory — that capital T Theory — that explains it is
bullshit as far as I am concerned. Sorry. That just drives me mad.
Wherever you name as having drawn theoretical input from —
that's where it is. (Excerpt from SOS transcript, February 1991).

As a doctoral student I could not not-jump at the door marked Theory, the
gateway to knowledge as understood within academia. It was assumed that
there was an askable question at the heart of my project and an answer to it
supportable by appropriate evidence. I was taught to foreground these elements and not to reveal the gaps in and around them. There were to be no
doubts, no inconsistencies, no spaces of wondering. There were distinct risks
associated with resisting this training: "The day they moved the door on me
my nose bled for a hundred hours" (White, 1990). Doing theory wrong gave
me some experience with psychic bleeding. Still, I was/am determined to
remain true to myself, my fragmented self.

My research refused to be unitary. Regardless of my desires, it would not
fit inside any particular intellectual tradition or theory. Gradually I came to

see that it existed in many different intellectual places including some pieces which remained within the liberal discourse from which it originated. My movement into other ways of thinking did not eradicate these roots. My acceptance of a multiplicity of views is a theoretical position as well as a political choice.[5] I rejected very little outright. I felt tremendous pressure from the Survivors of Sociology to focus specifically on subjectivity and the lived experience of consumers/survivors in policy development. As this shifting occurred in my work I felt a counter-pressure from David Livingstone, my doctoral supervisor, to create a political economy of consumer participation. He urged me to draw a line around the self-clarifying themes in the work thus avoiding the risk that it become a "sinkhole for subjectivity." His concern was, I believe, similar to Haug's on the matter of doing memory work, that it is necessary "to make connections between the everyday and the large context, while avoiding the vices of ignoring the totality and losing ourselves in untheorized details" (1992: 17).

I drew actively from all of these learning relationships. Doing so forced me to give up my addiction to intellectual integration in favor of juxtaposing the many different realities which are revealed through engagement with other people.[6] Lather puts it just right when she talks about framing "the varied critical discourses as differing practices and impulses that both weave together and interrupt one another rather than as fixed, contrasting positions" (1991: 19). Writing about class and education, bell hooks says:

> The most powerful resource any of us can have as we study and teach in university settings is full understanding and appreciation of the richness, beauty, and primacy of our familial and community background.... Education as the practice of freedom becomes not a force which fragments or separates, but one that brings us closer, expanding our definitions of home and community. (1989: 83)

In keeping things which others were prepared to discard as not new or politically correct, I reclaimed my prairie "conservatism." Retaining (some) male theorists and theory-making and coming to feminism was my version of "keeping close to home."

This choice was also about balancing "male" and "female" aspects of myself: masculine and feminine qualities. David Livingstone (DWL), and the members of SOS represented different sides of myself.

> Working through an SOS transcript I could see that I am claiming DWL to be preventing me, constraining me from a more feminist approach to the work when in fact I don't know that for sure. He takes positions/makes recommendations in keeping with his judgement. I often accept them — don't challenge them because they reverberate with the masculine in me.

Then I justify that by saying that he is insisting on certain things. In point of fact I don't have a strong sense of what he insists on because I haven't resisted his recommendations much.... Some aspects of my research are reproducing my relationships to men. What needs work here to change this is my feminine side — my confidence in it, assertion of it. (Journal entry, November 1990)

Part of my struggle to locate myself theoretically had to do with unresolved or conflicted gender identification, with the discovery and painful exploration of my own mysogyny.

KNOWLEDGE TOGETHER

The evolution of my knowledge over the past few years has been complex. However, all of my hard won intellectual attachments — connecting to sociology, taking up political economy, coming into feminism — have one thing in common. They are more than words on paper. They are shot through with subjective and interactive processes. For me, then, knowledge is social. It emerges with people's actions together and with their speaking about those actions. My worldview is distinct from that of other people who were involved in my project; speaking with my voice I bring their knowing into view. But the separation between us is at best temporary. This breaking down/breaking through is knowledge together.

NOTES

1. This shift for me personally parallels one happening in academic circles more generally. Lather (1989) terms it post-positivism. "Questions of how to do 'good' openly value-based inquiry can be seriously entertained, a discourse unheard of outside marginalized circles such as feminist and Freirean participatory research until very recently" (p. 12).

2. What I/the Framework project aspired to was a goal similar to that of critical pedagogy: "a critical democracy, individual freedom, social justice, and social change — a revitalized public sphere characterized by [mentally ill] citizens capable of confronting public issues critically through ongoing forms of public debate and social action" (Ellsworth, 1989: 300).

3. It has been easier for me to take up some threads of feminism and Marxism than others. The requirement that one must make explicit the forces and agents outside of immediate comprehension which shape both personal experience and policy has been difficult. It pushes against those aspects of this

project which remain rooted in liberalism and pluralism, which resist transforming the social and political system in which I live. Part of me is content with simply letting people speak. However as Schneider points out, Marxists and feminists "say it's fine to let 'them' speak but you must show how what they think and say and even who speaks at all are determined by 'larger social arrangements' — such as capital and patriarchy. And poststructuralists would say these discourses 'speak' the subjects" (1991: 309).

4. Kate isn't the first person to be put down by being told her writing was "journalistic." In 1957 Mills noted that "In academic circles today anyone who tries to write in a widely intelligible way is liable to be condemned as a 'mere literary man' or, worse still, 'a mere journalist.' Perhaps you have already learned that these phrases, as commonly used, only indicate the spurious inference: superficial because readable" (p. 218).

5. I have allowed myself to ask Britzman's questions: "What kinds of practices are possible once vulnerability, ambiguity and doubt are admitted? What kinds of power and authority are taken up and not admitted?" (1989: 17). My failure to invoke closure has its counterparts in Hutcheon's (1988) recommendation for ambivalence towards postmodernisms as a way of engaging with them, and of Johnson's (1987) and Spivak's (1987) recommendation for moving back and forth among contestatory discourses. Says Lather (1989), "Such interruptions can help us begin to sketch out what the 'not yet' is in our movement away from the 'no longer,' some outside of both the logic of binary oppositions and the principle of noncontradiction where we can 'reinscribe otherwise' while avoiding the fall into an infinite regress of demystification" (p. 8).

6. How successful can I be in giving up this addiction? Schneider points out that sociologists are taught to explain, translate and interpret, to look for general patterns beyond our own setting or case. It is difficult to unlearn this. "Even for theories that insist the researcher 'stay close to' and 'respect' the words and experiences of others — symbolic interactionism, phenomenological sociology, social constructionism — our analytic voice remains the ordering, authorial one" (1991: 306).

CHAPTER 5

Falling Off the Fence

All the King's horses
And All the King's men
Couldn't put Humpty together again

There has been a major shift in my participation in the community mental health field over the past five years. I understand this as, variously, becoming a translator between two worldviews, becoming fluent in two discourses, having my professionalism punctured, and falling off the fence. In this chapter I take up these images. I discuss the nature of that "fence," how I came to fall off and where I landed. Some of the discussion is in script form, a device which allows me to bring forward internal dialogue as an experiment in "deprivileging the omniscient author" (Lather, 1989: 9).[1] This "makes it easier to communicate emotion and moods as well as 'facts'" (Schneider, 1991: 303). Emotions are significant as I raise questions about how my life in categories such as "woman," "student," and "patient" is caught up with the regulation of my body and my relationships. This in turn revolves back onto ethical issues surrounding my engagement with survivors in research and gives rise to disturbing questions about surviving as a feeling person in a capitalist society.

SCHOOLED SUBJECTIVITY

While my CMHA "scars" were still fairly fresh I was part of a panel on the Canadian experience with partnerships for community care at the American Orthopsychiatric Association in New York. There I described for the first time what I thought the implications of "consumer participation" were for mental health professionals. I talked about having to "unlearn" many of the

51

ways I had been taught to relate to people as a professional and about initiating a new set of relationships. I located the origins of "appropriate professional behavior" within a process of peer socialization. I knew that the support and approval of one's co-workers is fundamental to success on the job. The direct involvement of consumers/survivors changed that process for me. Survivor ideas, needs and perspectives caused me to question my primary loyalties. I left the CMHA having raised but not resolved a fundamental question: Would I work in the interest of the organization which employed me, of the profession which trained me, or of the movement with which I had become engaged through the stories and lives of consumers/survivors?

I carried this question with me into OISE. There it became both less and more complex. Without fear of reprisal I could say that I was allied with the psychiatric survivor movement, that I felt no allegiance or specific identification with a profession or an organization, that I identified most strongly with people whose voices are silenced in society and with those who are prepared to break that silence. There was a healthy amount of room for the expression of these sentiments in OISE's academic environment. What was and continues to be difficult is the degree of personal change implicated in this shift. I read with interest that students in a class given by bell hooks:

> stated quite openly and honestly that reading the literature in the context of class discussion was making them feel pain. They complained that everything was changing for them, that they were seeing the world differently and seeing things in that world that were difficult to face ... learning to see the world critically was causing pain. (hooks, 1989: 102)

I was changing my life as an outgrowth of my engagement with psychiatric survivors. I could not contain these changes within my intellect or my professional life. Learning to see "consumer participation" critically caused me pain. More subtly, it caused me pain in an environment in which that pain could be neither acknowledged nor worked through. I found these circumstances intolerable.[2]

Breakdown!!?

> I am angry. I am angry. I am angry.
> (Journal entry, November 1990)

I am still angry. I know of few ways to deal with this feeling which threatens to overwhelm me, to immobilize me. My only hope is to drive it into my writing where there is the possibility that I can transform it into something which feels less personally destructive, which touches someone else and thereby breaks my isolation. I am reminded of David Reville's hospital journal:

> February 19, 1966: It works. But it works sporadically. The writing. Sometimes it gets me so high all the horror of this sitting room fades out completely. I feel competent, creative, energetic, invincible. But when it leaves me, oh, when it leaves me, I am at the bottom of the pit. I'm scared. And I can't even scream. (in Burstow and Weitz, 1988: 167)

Twenty-five years later I write for similar reasons. To escape my own horrors, to feel if not invincible, at least legitimate. Natalie Goldberg says that a writer must be willing to "sit at the bottom of the pit, commit herself to stay there, and let all the wild animals approach, even call them up, then face them, write them down and not run away" (1990: 29). This chapter calls up a forest of wild animals: In the heart of my engagement with psychiatric survivors I had a physical/emotional breakdown.

I need to write my "illness narrative" but I am very uneasy situating it as academic work (Kleinman, 1987).[3] My justification for proceeding is a feminist one. I accept and want to explore the contention that "the personal is political" (Weedon, 1987: 74). I believe that "breaking down" was inextricably wound up with my attempt to do activist research, to be political from within academia. It is also my most direct way of knowing about survivorhood. It reveals subjectively that which I have made the object of research. As Pettigrew says:

> All fieldworkers should feel justified in exploring their experiences and encounters in the field for, to the extent to which they have moved in rhythm with, touched the spontaneity of, and been near to and free with those among whom they lived, they have experienced the entry of another culture and another set of values into their own being. (1981: 78)

The radical shift in my being which took place during my research was expressed as illness and crisis. Writing about it makes me feel vulnerable but it is a vulnerability which "is no easy, sloppy or self-involved exercise in relating inner thoughts, feelings and fantasies" (Stanley and Wise, 1983: 197). My intent is not to psychologize my breakdown but to socialize it. Further than that I want to raise questions around breaking down. Breakdown? Who has broken down? Is she broken? Or is she together for the first time? I want to articulate how these questions have caused me to speculate about theory and how they suggest the experience of breaking through into fresh intellectual and personal ways of seeing.

Where does a breakdown begin? Choosing one point in time is terribly arbitrary. But since I must choose I will say that mine started with my encounter with Pat Capponi over a "survivor-directed Ph.D."[4] I have joked with her since that this meeting was so difficult it put me in the bathtub for three weeks. In fact it took much longer to come to terms with it. The doubts Pat had about my abilities were one thing. The open speculation about my "stunted personal development" was quite another. I know now that it is not unusual for Pat to do this; she believes in calling service providers personally to account. Other professionals have encountered her in inquisition mode and reacted differently. I suppose there have been people who smiled and shrugged it off. I couldn't do that.

Why couldn't I do that? In part it was because I took my project seriously. I took Pat seriously.[5] And it must be said, deep within myself I wondered whether she was right. While I was fighting to assert my trustworthiness, on a feeling level her words threw me into a chasm of self-doubt. What was the source of my legitimacy? Was I involved with psychiatric survivors to compensate for something missing or damaged in my own life? Was I in it for power? Or, as Lather (1989) might ask, was I contributing to dominance in spite of my liberatory intentions?[6] Unsettling questions for which I had no satisfactory answers.

At the time I was reading extensively about the political economy of Canadian schooling. In one text I came across the following words with sudden insight:

> To function (in a bureaucracy) either as a student or an employee means that emotionality (subjectivity) has been to a significant degree schooled out of you. "Excessively" subjective people find it difficult to play this bureaucratic role for too long. (Nelson, 1989: 123)

Here was one of the roots of my dilemma, part of the reason why Pat found me too cool and smooth, why she doubted my ability to work with survivors. She could not feel my subjectivity, my emotionality. It had been schooled into hiding. Becoming "educated" had given me the necessary skills for my project while simultaneously stripping me of the emotional attachments which would actually make it possible.

> suddenly realized Pat was right. My personal development has been stunted — by the very route that I had to use to escape the life laid out for me in Lacombe. Through education. It was my ticket out. Up to this point I have always thought of the years I spent in school as difficult but of the utmost value. This week I encountered the limits on my ability to act resulting from years of school relations.... I am attempting only now to liberate myself

from the obstacles of being educated. I must "unlearn" it. (Journal entry, March 1990)

I was ripe for feeling, emotionality, to flood back into my life. I was unprepared for how difficult it would be to live out the roles of student, organizer and researcher, from a feeling position.[7]

These changes caught me just as I began to follow the hearings into community mental health services legislation. I experienced my contact with consumers/survivors in this exercise with new depths of feeling for their triumphs and their tremendous pain. The experience forged connections with submerged parts of myself until I understood more clearly why I was drawn to their difficult worlds. Democratic rights. Equality. Justice. All of these. But for me as well as them. In my wallet I carry a small scrap of yellow paper dated June, 1990. It says:

> I have come to the topic of psychiatric survivors and their circumstances as part of a personal search for the roots of my own oppression. I learned to see it in their lives first. As a consequence (or a gift) I began to identify it and deal with it in my own life. Being female. Growing up on the periphery of the country. Being damaged by religion.

These were the hidden raw nerves which Pat hit with her remarks. My breakdown arose from these places of longstanding hurt and powerlessness which became unbearable as they were amplified by the pain I perceived among survivors.

Writing about feminist methodology, Duelli Klein states that in order to perceive what is happening researchers must open up "to using such resources as intuition, emotions and feelings both in ourselves and in those we want to investigate" (1983: 95; see also Hochschild, 1975: 281). I agree. But what must also be said is how destabilizing this will be, perhaps especially in the psychiatric area. In my reading I found only one other researcher who even hints at what can occur. In her ethnography of a community mental health program, Estroff reveals:

> In the process of struggling with this work I have actually experienced the urge and propensity to flee to psychic disorganization and disability — have felt the lure of craziness ... the experience has been a curious mixture of personal, intellectual and psychic turmoil. (1981: 4)

Over the course of this research I too have encountered "a potential crazy self well-hidden and shored up inside" (Estroff, 1981: 4). This is a frightening reality. Yet I think it is possible to take the experience apart and make something/s of it which Estroff did not.

Tissue and Tears: Illness Dialogue

> Sometimes my body leaves me,
> goes into another room and locks the door. There
> it bangs about
> like an angry thief....
> I don't know what sounds to make to call it back....
>
> Lorna Crozier, *Sometimes My Body Leaves Me*

Narrator: The roots of Kathryn's initial collapse lay within the pain and powerlessness which she perceived within herself and in the lives of the people around her. Any resources she had for coping with these feelings had been stripped away by the changes in her life precipitated by the move to Toronto. All that remained was a compulsive desire to keep functioning whatever the cost. The faltering of her body under the onslaught of her emotions, its varied expressions of her dis/ease, was a serious threat to that desire. She sought to remove the threat medically. After struggling through six months of skin problems which were unusual for her, she consulted a dermatologist who diagnosed the condition as "rosacea." In conventional medical terms this is "a chronic skin problem characterized by abnormally red nose and cheeks and sometimes forehead and chin (which) ... may feature acne-like pimples ... often runs in families and is most common in women, especially those with fair skin" (Berkeley Wellness Letter, 1992: 8).

1st voice: I am afraid to write this part. Afraid of the emotions that will rise up in me and with them the heat and pain in my face. So closely linked. But one of the things I am learning is that taking my terror in my hands and just jumping into it ultimately feels better than all my defence mechanisms.

2nd voice: (impatiently) Just give them the facts.

1st voice: (startled) I'll try. But it's like revisiting a nightmare which I'm not certain I've escaped from yet. I remember that in the summer of 1990 I was exhausted and run down. I spent days lying on the couch not sleeping but unable to get up and do anything. I wasn't sleeping well at night either. And I wasn't eating.

2nd voice: Sounds like you were depressed.

1st voice: Yes, I guess I was. But I couldn't acknowledge that. Looking back I can see that there was a tremendous letdown after the community mental health legislation consultation. I was going through some major emotional changes and I was really anxious about the stage I was at in my research.

2nd voice: So you had good reason to slow down for a bit.

1st voice: I know that now. I had uncovered some deep psychic wounds which needed tending. I should have permitted myself to be exhausted. I should have taken care of myself.

2nd voice: Don't be so hard on yourself. You sound like a sermon.

1st voice: Sorry. Sometimes that comes back on me. I have discovered that I don't have much compassion for myself. What I needed to do back then was take long afternoon naps, go to the movies, walk in the park, feed myself outrageous delicacies and hours of silence, spend time with friends.

2nd voice: So why didn't you?

1st voice: I was afraid !! Afraid of what I had discovered about my life. All these myths about myself which I could suddenly see as myths: that I had a happy childhood; that I felt connected to my family; that I was a good partner to Ross; that it was fine to be childless; that I liked being a woman; that I liked myself at all; that I knew what I was doing with my life and why. All the broken pieces of my life sticking out and named for the first time. My mind felt paralyzed and my body wouldn't work properly. I felt so alone. I panicked.

2nd voice: Panic has thick curly hair and large frightened eyes. She has worked on too many projects meeting other people's deadlines. She thinks she has an incurable disease. No one else has been able to confirm or deny it. She wakes up in the middle of the night pulling her hair out. She wants to dig underneath her skin and pull this illness out by its roots. She grabs at her scalp instead. She is crying for help but only when she is sure no one is around to hear her.

1st voice: I know Gendler's book too and yes, that's exactly what it was like (1984: 81). I didn't pull out my hair (although I know some women who have) but my skin broke out like it never has before in my life. And it wouldn't heal.

2nd voice: Lots of people break out when they're heavily stressed. It's no big deal.

1st voice: This wasn't a trivial or passing thing. Something was deeply wrong. My body wasn't behaving properly. It made me very angry.

2nd voice: Being angry at your own body sounds pretty counterproductive. It is *you* after all.

1st voice: I felt very alienated from it in some ways. Remember that I was just discovering the belief I held about the inadequacies of the female form, something I had hidden from myself for years. It was a very vulnerable time. And I had a lot of free floating anger which I didn't know how to handle. Anger about the pain of survivors, the inequities in the world, my own powerlessness. I guess I directed a lot of that back on myself.

2nd voice: Blaming the victim. What happened next?

Narrator: Most physicians attempt to control rosacea using oral or topical antibiotics. It usually disappears on its own but this may take ten years or more. They do not seem to have given much thought to the effects of a decade's worth of regular antibiotic use on women diagnosed with the condition. Kathryn was prescribed tetracycline and took it for six months. At the end of that time her situation was considerably worse. Her initial symptoms were definite but isolated. With "treatment" she developed serious systemic problems which were both physical and emotional.

1st voice: I was desperately trying to get some sense of control in the situation. I thought if I could just get my skin to behave I'd be okay. Just get the public mask back in place and the other stuff might sort itself out in time. So I did what I suspect a lot of people do in this situation. I went to the doctor. Or rather the dermatologist.

2nd voice: I have a bad feeling about this.

1st voice: And I am beginning to wonder who you are.

2nd voice: (evasively) Just tell the story.

1st voice: The dermatologist didn't think there was that much wrong with me. But she prescribed for me anyway. Antibiotics. Tetracycline internally and a cream.

2nd voice: (groaning) Not tetracycline!! That's terrible stuff.

1st voice: (dully) I took it three times a day for seven months.

2nd voice: Seven months !! That's outrageous.

Narrator: Gradually Kathryn's face turned a deep red. Bouts of facial flushing, familiar and previously fleeting, became frequent and painful with her increasing hypersensitivity to heat and light. She was almost constantly anxious and began to have regular panic attacks publicly and privately. Her teeth became very sensitive and began to turn black. Her entire face hurt and became sensitive to touch. The situation reached a crisis during a week-long trip which she and her partner, Ross, took to Mexico. In the airless, claustrophobic press of bodies on the plane she had a severe anxiety attack. Later, with only brief exposure to the tropical sun her face burst into blisters. She spent the "holiday" lying down indoors, talking through with Ross the almost irresistible urge to escape the pain of her own skin by drowning in the nearby Caribbean. She flew home under his watchful eye, sedated on Valium.

1st voice: I should have known that it was the medication.

2nd voice: What took you so long to figure it out?

1st voice: I wasn't thinking properly. I wasn't feeling ... anything. I got worse on the medication instead of better but I kept thinking "doctor knows best." By this time I thought there was something seriously wrong with me and that I really needed the medication to control it.

2nd voice: (indignant) There was absolutely nothing wrong with me that rest and love and the right kind of nurturing wouldn't have fixed. You bombed me with that shit!! I couldn't handle it.

1st voice: (even more startled) I know who you are! You are my body talking.

2nd voice: (grudgingly) It took you long enough.

1st voice: Well, I have a lot of trouble hearing you.

2nd voice: No kidding.

Narrator: A week after returning from Mexico, almost by accident and for the first time, someone read her the list of tetracycline "side effects" from the Compendium of Pharmaceutical Compounds. They include skin rashes, skin hypersensitivity and anxiety. The drug acts on the central nervous system; it penetrates the teeth and bones. It affects food absorption and results in photosensitivity. Long months of confusion cleared abruptly. Her steadily worsening physical condition was not the result of "rosacea" but of prolonged antibiotic treatment. She was suffering from drug toxicity severe enough to have resulted in deep inflammation of the facial skin, muscles and the linings of the bones. It was at this point that she began to make an emotional break with the ideology of modern allopathic medicine, rejecting not only the conventional treatment for "rosacea" but the very idea of it as a way of describing a bodily process.[8]

1st voice: I used to hear you better but that's gotten difficult since the move to Toronto. There's so much noise and distraction and so many demands on me. It wasn't until I came off the antibiotic and really started working with alternative treatments and in therapy that you started to come through again.

2nd voice: (singing softly) *I've got you under my skin. I've got you deep in the heart of me.*

1st voice: There's no need to be sarcastic. I'm serious about you now. A few months ago, half asleep, I became aware of the phrase "this howling place" and I knew you were still in agony. Some time later, during a treatment in the ozone bath I heard you say "I love this!" And I knew that in spite of how bizarre it looks to some people I'm doing the right things for you now.

2nd voice: For both of us.

1st voice: Yes. If it wasn't for good help and the people who love us we wouldn't be here.

2nd voice: The trip to Mexico was the absolute bottom. You wanted to kill me.

1st voice: Yes. Then and several times since. I didn't think that you could recover or that I had the patience to live through the agonies of it. Your being ill threatened relationships that are vital to me and put almost unbearable limitations on my life. I have so many things I want to do.

2nd voice: I know. I know. Places to go ... people to see.... You still have a lot to learn. But it was a big break for me when you really understood that you had poisoned me. You and that dermatologist.

1st voice: I had plenty of time to think about that last spring and summer. Lying in the dark because the light was too painful while the rest of the world drank iced cappuchino in outdoor cafes. I am barely able to get around even now.

2nd voice: (moaning) My poor eyes. My poor damaged face.

1st voice: It was sheer ignorance on my part. I was completely taken in by the medical model in spite of my insights to the contrary. But I am learning. Your pain is teaching me. Your aching bones. Your burning skin. They are my guides now.

2nd voice: You shifted the paradigm for yourself and forgot to take me with you!

Narrator: Kathryn extracted her body from conventional medical treatment and began to work with two health care professionals who take an expressive rather than suppressive orientation to working with bodies. She went into therapy with a woman who does bioenergetics. She came off tetracycline and committed herself to a process of detoxification with a physician/homeopath who uses a range of non-allopathic treatment methods. Her new physician viewed her skin problems as evidence that her immune and hormonal systems were profoundly out of balance. He introduced her to a controversial treatment called hyperbaric oxygen (ozone). Twice a week she takes two vials of ozone into her bloodstream intravenously. There it is converted to oxygen which makes for "clean" blood and less work for her struggling body. There is no scientific proof of the efficacy of this treatment. She can make little sense of it intellectually, so counter-intuitive is the notion of injecting herself with a gas. She began it in desperation and damage. She stays with it and justifies the cost of it because of the confirmation of bodily experience. It has been like running the tape of her dis/ease in reverse.

1st voice: Eight months so far we have worked through layers of tissue and tears. And more work to do yet. I am so sorry. Can you find it in your heart to forgive me?

2nd voice: We can talk about it.

My Crazy Reality

In a recent book about his own illness, sociologist Arthur Frank points out that "What happens when my body breaks down happens not just to that body but also to my life which is lived in that body. When the body breaks down so does the life" (1991: 8). By the time I returned from Mexico, the breakdown of the life lived in my body was extensive. For the first six months I experienced serious limitations to the most basic of my physical movements and daily activities. As long as I didn't put pressure on my face I could sleep; in the beginning I did that as much as possible. Awake, I had only about two hours early in the day when pain was tolerable enough to allow me to do anything; as the day progressed it deepened. Sunlight was a major enemy so I spent most of my days indoors lying down in the one air-conditioned room in our apartment. To get some exercise I walked early in the morning while the air was cool and the light less intense. If I had to go out during the day I criss-crossed the sidewalks seeking the protective shade of overhanging trees and buildings. The easing of these constraints was not a matter of days or weeks but months. As I write I hope that with the first anniversary of the Mexico crisis I will once again be comfortable in my body.

What I feel most strongly about being ill for a long time is how the process separated me from other people. I desperately wanted and needed company but I knew that seeking it would plunge me into hours or days of painful recuperation. On those occasions when I took the risk of, for example, having lunch with a friend I had unusual problems. Eating hurt because the pressure of chewing made my teeth and bones ache. The steam rising from cooked food fired my inflamed tissues. Talking was difficult because my facial muscles were contracted and the skin had lost its flexibility. I was deprived of the animation that goes with personal interaction; I was cut off from being touched. Usually it was only a short time before physical discomfort took precedence over my ability to be present to the person I was with and the pleasure of the encounter was compromised. But pain was only part of it.

The authors of an article on facial pain argue that those who suffer from it feel stigmatized; they feel estranged from and misunderstood by other people. A substantial minority believe that others attribute their condition to personality problems (Lennon et al., 1989). These findings are certainly true of me. My chief agony had to do with appearing in public; in social situations I could not reconcile myself to the ugliness of my appearance. I recently read David Jackson's account of falling apart after a heart attack and subsequent surgery. In it he says:

> Of course my time during the operation and then my later recovery in the intensive care unit are blurred, a confused time of severe physical disorientation and tearing, ripping pain. But what was significant was the way, not only that my external covering of hair was shaved off, but also that the protective shield of my historically constructed, masculinized body (the tensely held pattern that shaped my neuro-musculature) was smashed into and broken open. In the process of the heart surgery my chest was physically unzipped, my sternum broken and my heart repaired and reconstructed. I awoke with a new plastic valve busily and strangely clicking away inside me.... I really fell apart, emotionally, after the operation. (1990: 65)

The parallel took my breath away. His description gave me more words for the most deeply troubling aspect of my drug toxicity. According to one friend, I looked as if I had been irradiated. I felt mutilated. I didn't recognize myself; my original face had been replaced with a clown's mask. No amount of reassurance could change this perception. The damage was too deep. The changes in my appearance had destroyed the protective shield of my historically constructed feminine self-presentation to the world.

Models flaunt their flawless skins at me from countless billboards, magazine covers, and movies. I know the rules for women: look right, smile right, talk right (Hochschild, 1975). In spite of my own rational arguments to the contrary, I feel judged and condemned for failing to live up to standard, for becoming a woman who is not attractive. Self-loathing previously kept at bay overwhelms me. I feel that when people look at me what they see is my defectiveness as a woman. Who will love me now? There are answers from people around me but none from within myself. I systematically avoid mirrors and have trained myself not to look at my reflection in shiny surfaces. Intended simply to keep me from being immobilized by panic, this practice compounds my difficulties with other environments such as women's washrooms and the bright reflectiveness of the subway. It contaminates other practices which are bound up with images of femininity: getting a haircut; shopping for clothes; going out for dinner. All of these and more are part of the nightmare, part of the need not to look at having lost a face I can justifiably turn to the world.

My struggles with heat and pain made it necessary for me to curtail almost all of my activities. I stopped going into OISE. I withdrew from the Survivors of Sociology. I systematically called people and extracted myself from various projects and speaking engagements. I withdrew from conferences. I declined any requests which were made to me. I canceled a planned holiday with my parents. I declined social invitations except those extended by a small circle of friends with whom I had spoken in detail about my situation. This strategy was intended to give me the privacy I needed to recover. It became more than that when I was forced to confront the fragility of my identity. I now deliberately seek out the isolation that I had initially given myself out of necessity. I avoid face-to-face contact, keeping my eyes and head down in public, hoping I won't meet anyone I know and have to speak to. I come out only for certain people on certain occasions. I feel that I deserve to be alone. This is the full extension of the separations inherent in my illness. I moved out of the self who likes people and activity into a frightened withdrawn shadow-self who avoids people and does nothing but write. Pain. Loss of face. Immobility. Threats to intimacy. Relationship losses. Identity implosion. My life on the margins. My crazy reality.

THE COLLAPSE OF A LIBERAL HUMANIST SUBJECT

Take this waltz
it's been dying for years
Leonard Cohen, *Take This Waltz*

Most people would consider what I have just written as too personal for academic work. I have doubts about it myself. But what is the root of my doubt? I think about the split bell hooks experienced between her private and public selves when she wrote with self-disclosure, and about the connection she made from that split to ongoing practices of domination. I connect her observations with the contention that a partitioning of social space into private and public is central to liberalism (Bowles and Gintis, 1987). The public realm is considered to be the state while the family and the capitalist economy are private. The effect of separating these realms in this way is to exempt family and economy from the scrutiny of democratic norms. I know as a citizen that my crazy reality is supposed to be kept in "the family." I feel how even my limited attempt at consumer/survivor discourse violates the private/public partitioning of liberal thought which is definitive of the society in which I live. I expect some form of punishment. Why am I doing this?

According to hooks (1989), if we are to successfully challenge current forms of oppression and exploitation, we must talk about the points of connection where the public and the private meet. My breakdown is one of those points. The experience of losing control of my life is my most authentic connection to the psychiatric survivor movement. It has shifted the motivation for my involvement out of my head and into my body, into my rage about damage and suffering inflicted on individuals not violently and dramatically but casually in the context of the taken-for-granted. My glimpses of life on the margins made my knowledge of psychiatric survivors less abstract, less theoretical. They revealed the constructed nature of the differences between them and me. They shifted the internalized social processes whereby I construct them as Other; Other has become Me. From this place I have gut-level feelings for Jane W.'s inability to meet in a room if it was higher than the fourth floor of a building; Steve's need to pace just outside the door as a way of getting through meetings; Mary's flight into mania after becoming a consumer superstar; Laurie's giddy terror at working again; Dale Ann's struggle to come off valium; Ken's quiet courage in the face of his punishing voices; Pat's omnipresent black hat; Kate's still-bleeding wound over being the object of Grand Rounds; David's lingering sense of damage in spite of years of public and personal success.

Frank contends that medicine can diagnose and treat the breakdown of bodies but:

> sometimes so much fear and frustration have been aroused in the ill person that fixing the breakdown does not quiet them. At those times the experience of illness goes beyond the limits of medicine. (1991: 8)

I understand this deeply but also differently than Frank does because the most serious threat to my health was iatrogenic. My illness expresses the limits of western medicine. The dermatologist diagnosed my condition and treated it in a medically acceptable way. My body's response was to break down even further. Fixing this breakdown has required a radical rethinking of my body in which I have come to trust its intelligence over medical model explanations and practices.

> This practice of immediately going for a drug to relieve a symptom reflects a widespread attitude that symptoms are inconvenient useless threats to our ability to live life the way we want to live it and that they should be suppressed or eliminated whenever possible. The problem with this attitude is that what we call symptoms are often the body's way of telling us that something is out of balance.... If we ignore these messages, or worse, suppress them, it may only lead to more severe symptoms or more serious problems later on. (Kabat-Zinn, 1990: 277)

Acting as any citizen might in a health matter produced a disastrous outcome later on, deepening my crisis physically and emotionally. The fear and frustration arising from this dysjuncture will not be quieted. I will not quiet them.

Inside academia I was required to be largely a person of intellect and "doing academic work 'properly' depends upon a radical separation of mind and body ... forgetting our bodily knowing" (Dehli, 1991: 48; see also Rockhill, 1987). This reflects/reinforces a more general social requirement.

> The state of segregation of the feeling from the intellect and the detachment of the intellect from the will is one which is characteristic of the individual existing in the atomized state of contemporary capitalist society. (Pettigrew, 1981)

Illness as an outgrowth of an activist academic project changed this for me: "I couldn't go on imposing my conscious will on my feelings and bodily experience, ... I had to learn, however painfully, how to bring my feelings and my head together" (Jackson, 1990: 13). I no longer wish to take up my work or my citizenship in compartmentalized terms. I am seeking a standard for both which takes in my body, which connects my feelings to my intellect as a way of knowing.[9]

Taking Friendship Seriously

To be involved in the consumer/survivor movement, an individual must acknowledge publicly his/her personal history with psychiatric illness/treatment beyond non-stigmatizing forms such as personal growth therapy or marital counselling. One of the characteristics of Pat, David Reville and other psychiatric survivors in leadership roles is the extent to which they have gone public about their lives as psychiatric patients. For example, David's description of his life in Kingston Psychiatric Hospital has been in print in various forms since the late 1960s (1967; 1981; 1984; 1988). He has done what he calls his "ripping off my clothes speech" before hundreds of professional and survivor audiences over the past two decades. Pat frequently starts her public talks in a similar way; her story was published in the spring of 1992.

Professionals operate in the mental health field under exactly the opposite requirement. Professionalism is oriented towards objectivity, making judgements and decisions which are not "colored" by feelings, separating the private aspects of life from the public. When professionals and survivors work in "partnership," their rules for relating clash and the resulting dynamic is at best awkward. A survivor told me one day about his discomfort with the prerequisite round of introductions at service system meetings. All of the service providers in attendance give their name and their job title. He has the option of giving only his name, followed by an uncomfortable and uninformative silence, or stating that he is a psychiatric survivor. If he chooses the latter, he is the only person at the table who has volunteered any information of a personal nature. From this point on he feels disadvantaged and vulnerable in his interactions with the group. For a mental health professional, personal privacy, giving only "name, rank and serial number" in their involvements with consumers/survivors is a form of protection. This aspect of my life was punctured by my engagement with survivors.

Initially, any legitimacy I had in the mental health field came primarily from wearing the authoritative mantle of the Canadian Mental Health Association. Leaving that organization I stepped into David Reville's protective shadow as a first step in repositioning myself with consumers/survivors. His survivor credentials gained me admittance to that world as an observer, a "color commentator," and a "baby" advocate. It was Pat who challenged me to take the next step and reveal myself as someone who could be trusted in and of myself. Watching Pat and talking to her over the past couple of years it seems to me that trust/loyalty is her first issue — perhaps her only issue. She constantly asks herself: "Can I trust this person?" "Can I *still* trust this person?" "Where do this person's loyalties lie?" On what basis was she to trust me? When we first met, I believed that she should trust me on the basis of a credible work history — my public persona — and my connections. She found this vastly insufficient. She needed to have a sense of me personally. In our encounter over a "survivor-directed Ph.D." I learned that establishing trust between a survivor and a professional is not necessarily a comfortable or friendly process and that it can't be done in a situation where one person is expected to be personal while the other is allowed to remain public.

> Not until we begin to talk from our own dark recesses can we appreciate fully the risk for others as we, with the best of intentions, ask them to open up for us. (Rockhill, 1987: 13)

Being only public is voyeuristic (Rockhill, 1987; Ellsworth, 1989) and not in keeping with Oakley's operating principle: "no intimacy without reciprocity" (1981: 49). Some level of mutually negotiated self-disclosure is fundamental to the research relationship.

Pat would accept my involvement with her and the survivor movement only if it was reciprocal. Our relationship developed through personal disclosure outside of organizational or professional contexts and it wasn't easy. She is an urban working class lesbian radical survivor in a black hat; I am a heterosexual bourgeois intellectual from a small town in the prairie Bible Belt. Our initial conversations were facilitated by David's presence, by his ability to "translate" between us, and by our affection for him. Pat and David would talk while I listened. David and I would talk while Pat listened. Gradually Pat and I became conversant in each other's discourse. We learned the words and the topics which made it possible to speak to each other. The mysteries of the professional worldview. The behavior of bureaucrats. The rules of academia. Writing. Poetry. Love. Sexuality. On these terms we became friends. Through this and other relationships with consumers/survivors I have come to view friendship as a significant and legitimate basis for engagement in research with psychiatric survivors. What I am suggesting is that "science" as I perform it is as much about engagement as it is about explanation. It is about "a commitment to talk to and learn about each other and ourselves and to work out ways to respect and take each other into account" (Schneider, 1991: 308).

I am keenly aware that in coming to this position I have taken a serious (but not unexpected) fall off the fence of scientific objectivity. There is some comfort in the fact that I am not alone. Expressing a general principle of feminist academic work, Oakley suggests:

> A feminist methodology of social science requires ... that the mythology of 'hygienic' research with its accompanying mystification of the researcher and the researched as objective instruments of data production be replaced

by the recognition that personal involvement is more than dangerous bias —
it is the condition under which people come to know each other and to admit
others into their lives. (1981: 58)

Lather points out that "the combined voices of the varied feminisms, post-
colonialisms and marxisms have displaced an objective scientific reason
with a consciously political and social reason" (1989: 2). After examining
the dynamic played out around issues of race and gender in her own
classroom Ellsworth concludes that friendship is "an appropriate and acceptable 'condition' under which people become allies in struggles that are not
their own" (1989: 317). Lugones and Spelman (1983) reject self-interest and
theoretical/political obligation in favor of friendship as the only acceptable
motivation for following Others into their worlds.

"Working Together Across Difference"

If an "insider" and an "outsider" to a movement work together as friends, are
their interests identical? Clearly not. I remember the situation which clarified
that for me. In "Re/Membering Ourselves" I articulated a political position
which both Pat and I were comfortable with: that there is a basic we/they split
between providers and consumers of mental health services; that these
differences should be named; that a healthy recognition of separation is the
only acceptable basis for effective consumer/survivor participation. The
document wasn't even in print before we heard criticisms from a provider.
Our stance was "unbalanced," "biased" and "wiped out other people's
pain."[10] I was startled at that point to perceive how much my own location
within the mental health field had shifted. I felt my alienation from providers,
"my own kind." I was conscious of my emotional bond with Pat and the
constituency she represents but I felt with great clarity the various separations which made me different, which made my knowledge of survivors
partial. Like Ellsworth, I understood that:

> I brought a social subjectivity that has been constructed in such a way that I
> have not and can never participate unproblematically in the collective proc-
> ess of self-definition, naming of oppression, and struggles for visibility in
> the face of marginalization engaged in by [people whose survivor] posi-
> tion(s) I do not share. (1989: 309)

My friendship with Pat and our work together was not based on our similarities but on our comfort with naming differences. This possibility arose for
me out of my breakdown.

My crazy reality was diagnoseable. I was protected from dropping into the uncertainties of psychiatric treatment not by some hypothetical natural order or by strength of character but by the fact that particular structures in my life stayed solid and particular people respected my desire to take another course of action. Asymmetries of power and privilege cushioned my fall and continue to separate me from the full extent of what is possible when, for whatever reasons, a life comes apart. In this as in other experiences:

> Our differences are not just discursive or theoretical; they are material, embodied and political, as we struggle against or conform to modes of knowing and being in the world, as we learn to channel our desires in socially prescribed ways, but also as we continue to interrupt, disrupt, subvert, as we fail, run away, get sick, feel stressed, have breakdowns. (Dehli, 1991: 63)

I was never labelled, never admitted to hospital, never psychiatrically drugged, never given ECT. I was able to pay for alternative health care including a therapist who affirmed my feelings and reframed my situation as a positive process, a place to begin nurturing the ground of being. My housing remained stable and was a very real refuge for me. Ross, my partner, arranged office space for me in the nearby Toronto Zen Centre; there I began to write. Some friends disengaged but others took the opportunity to come close. The Survivors of Sociology kept in touch and understood my struggles as a promising rebirth. David Reville and Pat Capponi steadily reassured me of my sanity, gave expert advice on how to stay alive when you don't feel like it and had plenty of reasons why I should. Finally, and perhaps most significantly, Ross didn't turn me in. He listened to me, walked with me, read to me, fed me, provided me with financial stability and picked up the pieces of our life that I dropped. These are the resources which held me within the "normal" during that stretch of time when I could not live it. This is the place from which I know that my task with consumers/survivors is to "work together across difference" (Narayan, 1988; Ellsworth, 1989).

Falling off the Fence

Eight years ago I did intellectual work on behalf of psychiatric survivors from within the relative privacy of a job. I view this now as a position of privilege which I had to "unlearn" in order to be more emotionally and personally present in my relationships with people in the survivor movement. While crucial, this personal involvement is not to be taken lightly. Opening myself up to survivor pain was a significant factor in my breakdown. Arthur Frank's words keep coming back to me.

> After cancer I had no desire to go back to where I was before. The opportu-
> nity for change had been purchased at too great a cost to let it slip away. I
> had seen too much suffering from a perspective that is often invisible to the
> young and the healthy. I could not take up the same game in the old terms. I
> wanted less to recover what I had been than to discover what else I might be.
> (1991: 2)

I am discovering myself to be fragmented, to be many selves. My personal
work in therapy is not to fix this by somehow unifying myself but to accept
my own diversity, to know it and to allow all my voices to speak. Frank
describes how pain leads to the loss of order, loss of "a life that makes sense
as a fitting together of past and future" (1991: 31). My pain had that effect
on any number of levels including the theoretical and the political. In some
senses, the Kathryn who existed as a liberal–humanist subject came apart
along with the unified, rational and coherent world she lived in. I have been
able to come to terms with this, to experience it as more than loss, only to the
extent that I perceive it as a difficult but necessary clearing away of unwanted
barriers to a different sense of self and a different basis for my actions in the
world. In Natalie Goldberg's words:

> at some point in our lives we have to be crazy, we have to lose control, step
> out of our ordinary way of seeing, and learn that the world is not the way we
> think it is, that it isn't solid, structured and forever. (1986: 128)

My exploration of this position subjectively is what draws me to poststructural theories and their break with "totalizing, universalizing 'metanarra-
tives' and autonomous fully conscious stable selves" (Lather, 1991: 5; see
also Marcus and Fischer, 1986; Weedon, 1987; Britzman, 1989; Jackson,
1991). Losing this cohesiveness, I have been forced/enabled to begin constructing different selves/worlds. I have begun to stop feeling guilty for not
being a unified subject. I expend less energy covering over the gaps and holes
in my life. I can let down my masks. In turn, other people can do the same
with me, something which is crucial to my relationships with survivors given
the visibility of their chaotic subjectivities. For these reason I cannot view
my changes only or simply in terms of breaking down but must also view
them as breaking through.

NOTES

1. Mills suggested that sociologists "try to think in terms of a variety of view-
    points and in this way to let your mind become a moving prism, catching light

from as many angles as possible. In this connection, the writing of dialogues is often very useful" (1959: 214). People who have worked with dialogue, including scripted plays, in intellectual projects include Woolgar and Ashmore, 1988; Woolgar, 1988, 1989; Ashmore, 1989; Becker et al., 1989; Schneider, 1991.

2. I intend this as a general comment on educational practices. Whereas "Learning has always been depicted as this wonderfully positive experience ... it's not always. It can be downright wrenching, and move us into long periods of chaos and crisis" (Rockhill, 1987: 15).

3. Although it does not justify my approach theoretically, I take some comfort from being in good company on this one. In writing herself in, DiGiacomo (1987) worried about being considered "self-absorbed," "pretentious" or "nihilistic." She notes that Rosaldo (1989) invoked "personal experience as an analytic category despite the risk of being dismissed as sentimental and unscholarly." Rockhill's internal voices told her that introducing the subjective was "bordering on egocentrism, narcissism" (1987: 13).

4. Pat's comment after reading this is that perhaps I have given her too much responsibility for this experience in my life. This may be so. Certainly the account of my "breakdown" can be written in other equally valid ways than the way it is presented here. I am conscious of the risks for making what happened to me part of Pat's personal and "pedagogic burden" (Narayan, 1988: 37) and yet, for the purpose of illuminating certain feature of the relationship, I wish to let it stand.

5. Taking ourselves and other people seriously connects theoretically with the understanding that society reproduces itself in the details of everyday life (see Haug, 1992). It does not, however, necessitate a giving over of one's views or actions. I needed to take Pat seriously but also to understand her voice as partial. It needed to be problematized not to discount it but to make its implications explicit. Ellsworth puts it well in terms of teachers and students:

   > Students' and my own narratives about experiences of racism, ableism, elitism, fat oppression, sexism, anti-Semitism, heterosexism, and so on are partial — partial in the sense that they are unfinished, imperfect, limited; and partial in the sense that they project the interests of "one side" over others. Because those voices are partial and partisan, they must be made problematic, but not because they have broken the rules of thought of the ideal rational person by grounding their knowledge in immediate, emotional, social, and psychic experiences of oppression, or are somehow lacking or too narrowly circumscribed. Rather, they must be critiqued because they hold implications for other social movements and their struggles for self-definition (1989: 305).

6. Lather's question then becomes "What would a sociological project look like that was not a technology of regulation and surveillance?" (1989: 12) This is certainly something I have tried to answer for myself with this research.

7. Shifting discourses as I did had major implications for the ways in which I was subjectively put together; it necessitated emotional as well as intellectual change. As Weedon points out, "discourse constitutes ways of being a subject, modes of subjectivity which imply specific organization of the emotional as well as the mental and psychic capacities of the individual. After years of socialization and schooling these may prove hard to change" (1987: 98).

8. "Tissue and Tears" was written from inside the understanding of my body and my illness which I had eight month into alternative treatment. Now, more than three years into treatment, I would describe both in very different terms. Most of the symptoms I had when I went to the dermatologist were key indicators of environmental illness. They were misdiagnosed as rosacea and mistreated with antibiotics which contributed to further immune system breakdown. I continue to value the emotionality, the immediacy of the original account; the description is not false merely frozen in time. "Diagnosing" my "condition" is an ongoing piece of work which I engage in with my physician and my body. What I understand more and more as I do this work is that establishing a diagnosis is a hazy business, not at all as definitive it is made out to be.

9. Hochschild proposes for sociology what Jackson seeks as an individual. Making a case for a sociology of emotion, she suggests that "Roles and relations are surely not social patterns that apply only to thought and action, leaving feeling an untouched, timeless and universal constant. We must integrate the sociology of the 'head' with a sociology of the 'heart' and somehow erase the distinction in the process" (1975: 299). DiGiacomo notes that the Balinese have a concept loosely understood as "feeling-thinking" which blurs our own cultural separation of these modes of understanding.

10. There is a huge piece of liberalism lying behind this debate. The argument is that if survivors are given a chance to tell their stories, express their opinions, communicate their pain — then professionals must be given equal time. It's all in the interests of "balance" and "fair play." There is no recognition in this position of structural inequities, of the fact that when survivors speak they do so as tiny voices inserted into a cacophony of professional conversations, that the context in which they speak is already "unbalanced" in favor of professional voices. Poststructuralists argue that "There are no social positions exempt from becoming oppressive to others.... [A]ny group — any position — can move into the oppressor role" (Lather, 1989: 26, 27). Can it be that survivors could become oppressive to professionals as part of the dynamics of "consumer participation?" The suggestion seems wrong. Professionals may experience "consumer participation" as oppressive because of the implications it has for their own power within the system; individual professionals may suffer to some degree at the hands of individual survivors. However, some social positions are more likely that others to move people into oppressor roles. And being a psychiatric survivor isn't one of them.

CHAPTER 6

Disrupting the "Rational"

I have spent the past four years as a doctoral student studying and doing research into "consumer/survivor participation." In that time I have read a lot of books and articles looking for that special knowledge which would explain it all to me. After all of that I have learned one thing: that there is very little academic work which can prepare us for the dynamics of the real live situation which we all find ourselves in.

From my speech to "The Patient as Consumer"
Conference at Queen Street Mental
Health Centre, Toronto, April 22, 1992

There is a struggle going on in the mental health field to fix the meaning of "consumer participation" as "representation," something which would incorporate it into the dominant liberal political discourse. I propose a substantial (re)definition: that "consumer participation" is an "unsettling relation" (Bannerji et al., 1991). It is those practices which "unsettle" the comfort of mental health professionals in their relationships with psychiatric consumers/survivors. I have appropriated this notion from a book about feminist practice in which the authors attempt to disrupt power/knowledge relations within universities — including the places where they themselves are comfortable (Bannerji et al., 1991). I am engaged in a similar project within the mental health system: "leaving the comforts of home" aptly frames the changes which I have made and must continue to make as a worker.

Consumer participation as an unsettling relation makes much greater demands than "representation" does on both consumers/survivors and mental health professionals. It calls survivors into a process of self-knowledge whereby they can both *get angry* and understand the ways in which they *are being made angry* (Lyman, 1981). It then calls upon them to direct their anger

73

in ways which do not objectify professionals as "evil others," which move them beyond personal revenge into collective political action. The task for professionals is also difficult. "Consumer participation" as an unsettling relation isn't (just) a new program technique or an intellectual exercise. If there is any room at all for it to be genuine, it will engage people emotionally and personally; it will raise suppressed emotions and in the process challenge professionals' identities as "knowers" and "doers." Professionals must not marginalize these feelings, in themselves or particularly in survivors, for the sake of "getting on with business."

"Consumer participation" has the potential to call mental health professionals to account not just for how we do our work but for who we are. We should expect this process to be painful and conflictual. I realized this for myself the day after my fateful first meeting with Pat when I noted that "You don't have a genuine partnership until the screaming starts!" (Journal entry, March 14, 1990) However, if Pat hadn't risked being "rude" to me I would not have come to understand "consumer participation" in the ways that I do now. My friendship with her taught me that mental health professionals need to get curious about their own discomfort, to see it as "loaded with information and energy" (Lorde, 1984: 127). We need to get inside the dynamics of our conflicts in order to learn more about what is going on, to understand expressions of distrust or hostility as a necessary part of participation and not collapse in on our own needs in the face of them. In pain and conflict we encounter our deepest investments in the status quo and the strongest possibilities for divesting ourselves of them. I came to this position as a result of "breaking down," but it was more broadly confirmed for me when I analyzed participants' experiences during the provincial consultation on community mental health services legislation.[1,2]

THE CONSULTATION THAT GOT AWAY

Professional: I think the legislation consultation has gotten away from us in some ways. It has become bigger and more important than we ever expected that it would be and we have had to deal with that. It hasn't always been easy. But I think that consumers have presented viable options and challenges to the way that we have done things.

Survivor: I think they fucked themselves. Whether their intentions were lip service or what, the door was open and we won't let it close. So I am not too worried about what motivated them. I

suspect it wasn't the best of motivations. Too bad. We saw the
window of opportunity and we kicked it in.

The legislation consultation was sponsored by the Ontario government in
the spring of 1990. It was the largest formally — sanctioned "partnership"
exercise between psychiatric consumers/survivors and mental health professionals in the history of the provincial mental health system. All of the
professionals involved in this initiative were supportive of the idea of
"consumer participation" but its meaning and significance differed amongst
them. Those in senior bureaucratic positions were oriented to it as an
established health policy aimed at managing health care costs through decen-
tralized planning and decision-making. They cited relevant literature as well
as federal and other provincial initiatives in support of it. "Consumer participation" came under the heading of "good business practice" or "quality
management" and as such was not perceived as a threat to the system.

Professional: You have to talk to the people you are supposed to be serving.
It's quality management whether it is building cars or providing services or making hamburgers or delivering mental health
services or services to women or to francophones.

Professional: It is the in vogue thing to do. And because it has been taking
place and people are beginning to see value added they are
becoming convinced that it is a good thing.

Further down the hierarchy, a sense of discomfort began to appear.
"Consumer participation" was interpreted as "representation" which meant
that actual people had to be attached to it. Mid-level bureaucrats were
prepared to accept this just as long as those representatives participated
according to the established rules. Particularly strong was the requirement
that consumers/survivors chant The Professional's Mantra:

balance contribute constructive participate broader perspective
effective planning patterns systems logical sense order viable
options responsive responsible manage cost research solutions
coordination mechanisms linkages structures frameworks
integration dovetailing functional strategize cohesive
encompassing larger directions range of issues common ground
productive corporate interface appropriate parameters pragmatic
useful concrete accurate valid

Several of the professionals who were involved perceived "consumer
participation" as evidence of a government bias against service providers.
Those who felt this most sharply framed their concern as a plea for "balance."
They viewed a strong consumer/survivor constituency as a threat to oppor-

tunities for unified action amongst those groups attempting to advance the "community" sector.

> **Professional:** I am beginning to think that we are getting into three new solitudes with the consumers going one way, the professionals going another and the families going another. What we are losing is the chance for any kind of unified advocacy in the province. And if we lose that the government is likely to turn its attention in other directions.

> **Professional:** The philosophy and the value that the government gave earlier in the system about getting consumer involvement went too far to one end of the continuum.... I am worried about a splintering, fragmentation of consumer interests to not-consumer interests.... Things cannot and should not compete with each other.... There will be losers and the name of the game is not to have any losers in the system.

This perspective was offset somewhat by professionals who viewed "consumer participation" as a tool for reorganizing the system politically, although activating it within the "community" sector was perceived as a rather limited strategy.

> **Professional:** I have a lot of sympathy for community service providers. I think that is the right way to go. A number of them are doing the wrong things and well-intentioned do-gooders are probably very dangerous people. But I don't think they are as dangerous as psychiatrists and people with entrenched power. It doesn't really help in the end to alienate everybody.

Finally, for some mental health professionals, "consumer participation" was a process which engendered personal conflict. It was confusing, unexpected, even frightening. They struggled to make it fit inside their world. They were converted to it. They were silenced by it. It made them question what they knew and how they acted. It "unsettled" them. The closer a professional was to direct, sustained involvement with psychiatric survivors in policy-making, the greater the chance that s/he had been unsettled by the contact. The legislation consultation generated numerous opportunities for this to occur; crucial interactions took place between professionals and survivors which made it less possible for those professionals to live the social relations of the system without reflecting on them. Several points of interaction were particularly significant. They featured survivor struggles to be adequately represented and supported as consultation participants, to redefine the consultation agenda and its code of behavior, and to shape the legislation committee's final report.

Getting to the Table

When the legislation committee was first established, it drew two representatives from advocacy organizations but had no direct consumer/survivor members. The advocates made this an issue for the bureaucracy by refusing to constitute consumer/survivor representation.

Professional: When the committee was struck it didn't have any representation on it. My recollection was that MBV certainly raised this as an issue.... I thought "Oh, another screw up. No consumer representation." There was a lot of discussion about who that representative or those representatives should have been.... We would have had a roundabout discussion where names were put forward.

Professional: I didn't understand the politics. In hindsight now it was an omission. It wasn't a conscious attempt to keep consumers out. It was just that it wasn't in the bureaucratic file drawer. It could have been remedied easily by "Look, let's get someone." ... Anyway it did happen. A little late. They should have been there from square one. It is totally bizarre that the bureaucrats didn't think about that.

Professional: I am not quite sure how that happened ... but I think what they did was put out the call to the Advocacy Resource for the Handicapped. And ARCH said "We have put people on your bloody committees forever and we are really tired of it. It drains our resources and the reports sit on the shelf and we don't see any benefit to us, unless you want to pay them" and that didn't seem to be in the cards. So they sent DD. He and MBV spoke out in favor of real consumer participation. They said from the outset, together and independently,... "We don't want the presence of advocates to be taken as consumer representation. We are not consumers."

Professional: From the start there was not really the intent to have people there. While the rules talked about consumer input, the unwritten rules were that doesn't really mean consumers. Once we got beyond that there were some attempts at control over who got appointed and how and why.

The incident which put an end to the fumbling and indecision on this matter took place on a hot day in June 1989. The Deputy Minister of Health was touring a drop-in center in Toronto's Parkdale district when Pat Capponi "laid it on the line" with him about the need for survivor representation. He responded with air conditioning for the sweltering Centre and by giving the green light to her membership on the legislation committee.

The bureaucracy did not expect the discussion of community mental health services legislation to become contentious.

Professional: The view at the time was that legislation was probably going to be dry and technical. People thought this would be a navel-gazing, rational kind of research exercise to pull together all of the other legislation.... If you look at who composed that committee earlier there were lawyers and a few people from a previous committee, a lot of staff from government. It was going to be a pretty technical exercise: "Let's not get our hopes up here."

Professional: The terms of reference were that they were going to develop a document, they were going to hold consultations and they were going to make recommendations to the Ministry of Health. A number of people thought that we were going to have a draft Community Mental Health Act for our report. That expectation just got dropped along the way, mainly by the committee members. They weren't told not to do that but I think they felt progressively less able to deal with it.

Its gradual transformation into a dynamic process owed much to Pat's presence and her relentless survivor agenda. Her chief concern once she became a committee member was to bring in more psychiatric survivors, particularly since the committee intended to do hearings. She knew that it would be difficult for her to do that process alone. Believing that she had struck a deal for two more representatives, Pat put the offer to Toronto Psychiatric Survivors and came up with four volunteers. Meanwhile, formal approval for the increase was not forthcoming. This was a threat to Pat who already felt that she had gone out on a limb to involve survivors in a process for which there were no guarantees. Feeling heavily responsible and concerned for her credibility, she took steps to deliver the terms of her deal. From her office at the Gerstein Crisis Centre, she faxed "one of those 20 point letters" to the Director of Community Mental Health and to the Coordinator of Mental Health. She was offered a meeting at which the three women involved negotiated their way out of the conflict: Pat got her two additional representatives. From this point on, Pat's concern shifted to securing support for the survivor representatives and for survivors making presentations before the committee.

As plans were made for travelling to the various hearings, conflicts developed over which survivors were going where and how their attendance would be paid for. Rooted in her personal knowledge of poverty, Pat pressed the organizers to advance survivor committee members sufficient funds to cover the costs of their involvement. However, the bureaucracy was set up to reimburse people for expenses; the rules tacitly presumed that everyone was basically well-off. Heated exchanges over train tickets, taxi chits, hotel and restaurant bills threatened to derail the consultation before it got well underway.

Professional: There were all kinds of incidents that occurred over the organization of the thing during the consultations themselves that really set the committee members' teeth on edge and got everybody quite alienated throughout the process. Everybody was mad at everybody else.

Survivor: It was a struggle getting the guys up front money so they didn't have to use their own money and may not be able to make the rent.... They didn't send the guys cabfare. They didn't send them their train tickets on time. To register in a hotel is very difficult with no credit cards. People were worried about what was chargeable and what was not. Survivors aren't free enough to grab a cab to go to an airport. That is serious money. To get meals in a hotel is serious bread. And they were supposed to wait something like three to six months to get that back? !!

Pat reads an individual's attention to the details of another's oppression as a fundamental measure of the seriousness of his/her political commitment. Thus, she viewed bureaucratic struggles to provide instrumental support as insensitive and gratuitous hurt inflicted on vulnerable people. Not all of the survivor representatives shared this orientation.

Survivor: Why the hell is so important whether somebody made a mistake at the hotel desk and called somebody at the wrong time in the morning or some goddamn thing. Give me a break! I don't care.... That is not what I am here for ... don't care what you pay me, I don't care what the travel arrangements are.... We are supposed to be listening to people's pain.

However, Pat was taken seriously when she threatened to walk out over the issue of arrangements. For their part, bureaucrats at several levels were desperately trying to learn how to provide support while hemmed in by structural barriers which frustrated them almost as much as they did survivors. There were internal battles over the issue of getting consumer/survivor expense checks made up ahead of time. Eventually, the limited money available for the consultation was "bootlegged" through community agencies. In the interim, bureaucrats paid for survivor expenses using personal credit cards, hoping to be reimbursed themselves later on.

Professional: You see incredible mistakes and when you look back you can't imagine how you did it. I remember telling someone they could have this hotel room. It never occurred to me that they would think they had to pay for it, that they wouldn't just sign it and it would get billed like everybody else. Things were not done in any kind of malice or nastiness. Just stupidity.

Professional: I knew that I was getting up early. I was doing things for these people that I wouldn't do otherwise and yet just not quite doing it right and not quite figuring it out.... The organization is so bad at dealing with these issues that they put us in a bad position. It was all really unfamiliar territory.

Professional: We tried to brainstorm and come up with some ideas that might keep the consultation moving and not allow it to bog down entirely in some of the practical things that were making consumers feel that it was difficult to participate. It was my first time. It was the Ministry's first time. For many of the individual staff involved it was their first time.

Shifting the Agenda

The trouble with the public hearings extended beyond "the practical things" into the structure of the sessions themselves. Pat was concerned that consumers/survivors would be too intimidated to speak out in forums which were heavily populated with professionals.

Professional: I think the major issue of the consultations was a lot of debate about how they were going to be structured because Pat was very busy with you and with David organizing all this participation. She was very careful to make sure that it wasn't going to be structured so that people couldn't participate.

In response to her concerns, the legislation committee recommended an arrangement for the hearings whereby survivors and family members in each of the seven regions would have an informal session with the committee separate from the main body of presentations. Survivors were not precluded from making presentations as part of the regular agenda but there was also a separate space for them.

Meanwhile, David Reville was concerned about what constituted "the agenda," with the way in which the legislation committee shaped the issues it brought forward for public discussion. Some of my own organizing enters the picture here. I discovered that the consultation had been convened much too quickly for people to find out about it and to prepare themselves to participate. The thought of discussing legislation, especially in a public forum, was intimidating to service providers and consumers/survivors alike. There was a consultation document but the legislation committee itself was unhappy with it. At the request of high level bureaucrats, it had been rewritten to eliminate specific recommendations in favor of fourteen general questions. Many people and groups either hadn't received the document or were finding its contents complex and vague. A surprising number blamed themselves for this, assuming that the issues were beyond their comprehension. For this reason, David sent his own message on parliamentary stationary to a large number of groups and individuals across the province.

> Come to the hearing.... Make a presentation. There is time set aside for us. Tell your own story. You could put in a written brief, too, if you want. Don't worry about the questions in the discussion paper. If the questions don't interest you, leave them. Say what you want to say. (Letter from David Reville, Member of Provincial Parliament, to consumers/survivors in the province, March 1990)

It is difficult to gauge the impact of this attempt to give consumers/survivors both the opportunity and the permission to speak. What is clear is that survivors attended the legislation consultation in unprecedented numbers and that their comments, however brief or unprepared, raised issues which had not been on the legislative committee's original agenda, issues which were originally excluded as "horror stories."

Survivor: He said that he didn't want to hear horror stories: "I don't want to hear any horror stories. Answer the questions as they are laid out." You know, those stupid questions.

The broadening of the discussion was viewed by some as a disturbing failure to "remain specific to the task" at hand; others viewed it as the right place to start.

Professional: I saw something last night that doesn't happen in our valley. I saw people speaking out. And if you don't listen to these stories then all that you are doing here is wasted.

Gradually, two distinct streams of discussion arose within the consultation, one engaging mental health professionals and the other engaging consumers/survivors. With some exceptions, professionals addressed the issues as they were framed by the consultation document. They talked about decentralization, regionalization, local authority, mandates, funding mechanisms, treatment models, professional autonomy and target populations. They were On Topic. Consumers/survivors were not. They did not discuss legislation. With one or two exceptions, they talked primarily about their experiences of the mental health system and their lives in the community. They talked about hate, prejudice and poverty, about self-help, capacity and power, about loss, suffering and struggle. They asked to be included. They cried. They paid tribute to each other.

In our initial encounter, Pat shocked me with this same kind of communication. She brought the personal into a "public" discussion, something which I had been taught both at home and at school never to do. Only recently have I come to understand this not as "bad manners" ("in poor taste," "low class") but as, potentially, a political act which circumvents stratifications built into patterns of communication. I learned this for myself when I incorporated personal narrative into my doctoral dissertation, something which put me at risk for professional censure. Bringing the private and personal into the public/institutional is the mark of a survivor; it is a survivor strategy for transforming the institutional. All of the survivors I interviewed have done this with varying degrees of "success." With some it contributes to their continued disempowerment; with others it is the touchstone of their liberation.

Debating "Proper" Behavior

The ongoing battle over the consultation agenda was augmented by a major debate which grew up over the "right" way to behave. On the survivor side of things, Pat was haunted by a persistent concern that professional members of the legislation committee did not know how to communicate with her people. She was tremendously worried about the hurt that survivors might sustain at the hands of insensitive professionals. She felt that committee members had to learn what to say and what not to say to survivors, how to talk to them. It was out of this concern that the "sensitization" sessions were born.

Before the public hearings were held, the members of the legislation committee met with a group of five consumers/survivors in the informal surroundings of one committee member's home. Pat was paid to choreograph the event; she in turn paid her survivor presenters. Committee members worked through a series of prepared questions in small groups prior to listening to the survivors tell their stories. It was a tense situation for those who had never "testified" before.

Survivor: I had never presented in public before.... Two seconds into the thing I knew "Well, obviously they don't want to be bothered with us.".... I wondered why these people wanted to hear this about my life. I don't know if it was respect. It was listening. It was courteous. No one had any questions. They nodded. They looked down. They looked around.... It was a hard work doing it. It was so hard and painful. I guess that came through because everybody just sat. I am a private person. I don't like to do this sort of thing.

The committee handled this situation with great care, being generally very positive in their review of the experience. This response is a good measure of how much authority the issue of "consumer participation" began to command once there was a vocal psychiatric survivor on the committee working with bureaucrats who had orders not to let the process fall apart.

Professional: I have a very positive feeling about those sessions.... Initially I was a bit uncomfortable because they started off being confrontational and provocative. However, by the end of the evening I felt that it had really helped develop my own appreciation of the point of view the consumers/survivors bring to these situations.

Professional: I liked the criticism. There was a lot of good criticism, supportive criticism and comments and the sense that both sides had an opportunity to say something.... For me it was a good experience.

Professional: People were on good behavior I think.... I quite enjoyed the sessions.... It was interesting because people were on record. People said things there that they basically had to be held accountable for during the rest of the process.... I don't think it would have been easy for anyone to have been a dissenter there.... It established Pat as a leader in terms of the committee functioning....

The more experienced survivors felt strongly for their companions who had spoken publicly and powerfully for the first time about their psychiatric experiences. They also pondered the meaning of the sessions strategically.

Survivor: It was fraught.... Some of the sensitizers were very nervous about this situation.... The environment was chosen to be more relaxing but it was probably less relaxing than a more neutral boardroom space would be.... It was quite extraordinary. One of the presenters spoke for the first time about some sexual abuse that had occurred. The committees were very well behaved. They were polite and participated cheerfully in the tests that had been invented for them. There was extraordinary patience displayed by the professionals.... I view it almost as patronizing myself. In fact it is a kind of a "Guess Who's Coming To Dinner" thing....

Survivor: I have been wondering if it was a mistake. To me one of the millions of ways it might have been relates to that theory that you don't let a wheat shipment in if there is famine because famine can breed revolution. So do you let them go and be so awful to our folks? But it wouldn't have gone beyond one meeting because I couldn't stand it. I wouldn't be able to stand it.

For their part in the debate over behavior, professional members of the legislation committee were uncomfortable with Pat's tendency to confront professionals on the substance of their public presentations. Her stated agenda was to get at the facts. The committee was to collect information which would form the basis of its final report. Therefore it seemed logical to her to check on the information. However, this was viewed as "grilling" presenters — improper behavior for a committee member. She was told she was intimidating presenters; professional members of the group pressed her to be more "reasonable" in her dealings with the people who appeared before them.

Professional: On at least three or four occasions X pulled the subcommittee out and said "We are here to listen, not to contradict, not to argue, not to dialogue. We are here to listen to what people say." The only element outside of that was to provide some support to people who were very nervous in speaking. Either consumers or family members because both groups had people who broke down.

Survivor: We could ask questions but the only kind of questions we could pose were of a particular kind. We could ask them to clarify what they were talking about. We didn't have the right to editorialize or anything like that.... Clarification.... And no editorializing.

The other survivor representatives were concentrating on listening, one primarily to fellow survivors, the other to a broader range of voices.

Survivor: I zeroed in on the opportunity that our people, survivors, had to bring forward their stories or recommendations. No one had ever listened to us before. I was going to make sure that every survivor who wanted to talk had an opportunity to talk. And if I had to sit through professionals I would do that too....

Survivor: I still think that anybody who was there and who heard the words and who heard the people and who talked to them and who asked the questions and who was awake, went on the goddamn trips and had their expenses paid was duty bound to listen to them. We had a responsibility to listen to those people whether they were service provider or survivor ... or whoever. We had a responsibility to listen whether they have never done anything imaginative in their life. We had a duty to treat them as democratically as we could and to listen to them. And we didn't. As a group we did not.

This entire dynamic was understood by some participants as control attempts operating within the consultation through the taken-for-granted practices of established meeting behavior.

Survivor: Control attempts were utilized. They weren't particularly sophisticated and they weren't particularly effective. They were the kinds of control attempts that are fairly familiar where you restrict the amount of time and you create a sort of artificial process which reduces the likelihood of messy, chaotic consumer/survivor behavior.

Professional: There were the usual types of control about what it is appropriate to say and not to say and who it is appropriate to address it to and the reasonable channels that you go through doing things and so on. I am not suggesting that they were set out specifically for this committee to stop consumer participation but they are there as the rules which most of us are used to operating on committee.

Shaping the Final Report

When the consultations were almost over, the legislation committee sat down to talk about what to do next. There was confusion and dissention over how to produce the group's final report and over what kind of a report it should be. Committee members had at their disposal transcripts of each of the seven public hearings as well as written submissions from people and groups all over the province. The problem was how to make use of this massive amount of material. Working groups were struck to look at major areas; people went off to write papers. However, very few were actually able to do the writing. Committee input was uneven, unpredictable and slow. Group members gradually realized how big a task writing its report was. They decided that resources from outside the committee were required if the job was going to

get done. Appointed members to the committee thought that having bureaucrats draft the final report meant giving away too much power. And so the
final report wasn't written by the committee, its chair or its staff. Instead,
consultants were brought in to do the job. This was only partly satisfactory
in mitigating committee suspicions as it was bureaucrats who met regularly
with the consultants to review the writing in progress.

Committee attention shifted from process to content. For their part, the
psychiatric survivor members were eager to stick to the transcript material,
to see that the final report responded to the consultations — the arena in
which they had scored major points. But the writing of the final report was a
fresh battleground. Professional committee members saw the consultations
as one source of data and presumed that other research and literature should
be brought to bear in shaping the final report. When it came to the task of
formalizing recommendations, some of the professionals who had earlier
been willing to let some issues slide started to take tougher stands. Fax
machines began to hum.

> **Professional:** I think the consumer/survivors used the committee process
> because that was their vehicle. That was when they had our
> attention. When we were writing the final report, service
> providers were able to produce a paper and turn it directly into
> the consultants. They had the fax machine to get things back
> and forth faster. They had greater access to the people who
> were actually writing the report at the end.

Gradually, there was a break with the public hearings and the transcript
material. People reverted to the interests they represented as their primary
reference point rather than using the collective process which they had just
been through as a new starting point.

> **Survivor:** Essentially what we did was ignore the transcripts.... We
> responded to the internal transcripts, welded those together
> with our old tried and true positions from wherever we came
> from and went merrily off in a hundred different directions
> creating more gaps than already existed. And then attempted
> to plaster them over. We were trying to cover earthquake
> fissures with polyfilla. That's what we were trying to do with
> the mental health system.

While a tremendous amount of "conviction" had developed around the
consumer/survivor message it had not become definitive. Survivor representatives had to re-insert issues such as housing and jobs into committee
discussions on the final report. They viewed their professional "partners" as
too system focused and protective.

Survivor: We started meeting at the McDonald Block down at Bay and Wellesley. Simply haggling over what each of us thought was important and trying to fit this much into this much space. We were all working obviously for ourselves, for our people.... I felt that my job was done and was prepared to give it over to these people — which was a big mistake. Then I realized that this is where it counts. I remember Pat going, going, going, for housing. We started out with "This report is what we are going to do for survivors." In the end it was just trying to get one in here and one in there.

Survivor: The issue is making sure we don't apologize for the past, that we don't whitewash it, that we don't pretend that we conducted a marvelous process. We don't want to insult people by implying that housing is fine. We don't want to limit what we are going to say to the shrink in the hospital, to hospital beds or community programs because people's lives are more than that. We don't want to pretend that we have a partnership because we don't. We can't have any equality until people are helped to be equal and strong.

Survivor: They are coalesced around saving their ass. Saving their jobs. Saving the traditional system. Their focus is the mental health system. They will sit there and look at you straight in the face and say "We all want the same thing. Why can't you see that?" And I keep saying or want to say "Because you are lying. That's why I can't see it." I can't see it because it isn't there.

By the close of the legislative committee deliberations, survivors and others had succeeded in ensuring that the final report took a rights approach to the issue of legislation; service system issues were not front and centre. From the professional point of view this is a serious weakness.

Professional: I think there are a number of recommendations that just won't fly. There will be some things that will be completely ignored. My hope is that it will go on to a drafting of legislation and that the most salient parts of it as far as actual community stuff will get into legislation. I also anticipate that there will be a great hue and cry from doctors and union members if it goes forward so that in fact it may not go forward.

Professional: You have got to look at the systemic issues more. The report doesn't talk enough about how you are going to change the system.... There isn't a lot in there around systems. And I don't know if this was the right group to do that so I am hoping we still have a chance to do that. Because that is where you talk about funding and dollars....

Survivor: I know that some elements are delighted about the rights part and some people in the bureaucracy are unhappy about the service system part and the structural part because they think it is quite vague. The other question is what is the real effect of the report? How will it get translated into legislation and what will happen programmatically anyway?... I think one of the things that is very hard to visualize is what the policy development process really is like. The agenda is very crowded. The agenda is crowded with all sorts of difficult problems and quite frankly community mental health legislation isn't on the political agenda at all.

The final report of the legislation committee was submitted to the Ministry of Health in February 1991. It wasn't formally released until May 1993. Action specific to the committee's recommendations has not yet been taken.

DEEP STRUCTURE

These stories of the legislation consultation are a powerful contrast to most academic literature on policy-making. Academic accounts portray policy-making in distant and abstract terms. They make the process appear orderly, rational and linear; if they are peopled at all it is by cognitive beings only. Academic accounts do not describe the dynamic interactions which I both observed and was part of during the legislation consultation. They do not reflect what I know about how people actually live "policy-making." Lived policy-making is characterized by serendipity, by sudden, irrational changes and unexpected, unpredictable events. It is full of actual thinking and feeling people doing actual jobs — people I know or know of as an "insider" to some pieces of the process.

These stories are also a powerful exemplification of Weedon's argument that, by focusing on "narrow legal and constitutional definitions of individual freedom," liberal democracies "are blind to the deep structures of inequality between individuals. The exercising of power in these societies is, therefore, largely invisible" (1987: 120). There is a chasm between mental health professionals and psychiatric consumers/survivors which is not resolved by representation, by simply including consumers/survivors in activities and processes from which they have previously been excluded. It is not resolved by their formal presence on boards, at conferences or on government committees, as essential as this may be. Even as they sit across the same table from each other, professionals and their survivor "partners" are profoundly divided.

Warner suggests that, to the extent that community participation in any health issue is driven by a grassroots groundswell, it will be "an unpredictable force introducing an emotive element into the planning process" (1981: 355). I encountered a powerful surge of this "emotive element" within myself as I worked with psychiatric survivors, and in both survivors and mental health professionals during my investigation of the legislation consultation. Emotions were the deep structure of inequality within the legislation consultation; power was exercised invisibly within the committee and the public forums through emotional socialization (see Giroux's discussion of Bordieu, 1983: 270).

Dialogue: Hearing So Much

Survivor: In one consultation we had closed sessions, one for survivors and one for family members. And the survivors talked about the local hospital.... There was so much pain. I guess I was glad in one way that they could talk about it. Maybe that would help them.

Kathryn: The stories were pretty grim.

Survivor: At the same time I was not wishing I was somewhere else. I was committed to being there but I just heard so much, you know?

Kathryn: Yes. Well, it would reverberate back onto your own pain too I would think. That would be the hard part for me I know.

Survivor: The families were in as much trouble as the survivors. One woman's son had committed suicide the week before. She was a native mother of twins who are both schizophrenic. For the first time I realized that families certainly have legitimate concerns. I am not questioning our freedom of choice or anything like that. I am simply saying that families should group together for comfort.

Kathryn: So it really exposed you to a whole other layer of mental health issues. And what about the service provider piece of it? How did you cope with that?

Survivor: Well, a lot of the time I was listening but I don't know where I was. It depended on the speaker I guess. There was one speaker who was a psychologist. He spoke about how we could have helped in the past. He almost sounded suicidal; he was so depressed. This was a service provider! I wanted so badly to go over and say "What's wrong? What happened?" Because he was hurting so much.

Kathryn: You were really deep into it.

As a teller of tales, I want to bring policy-making to life by connecting challenges to the knowledge/power forms of policy-making with the expression of particular emotions. The legislation consultation was characterized by a tension between the emotional turbulence of participants' experiences and a code of professional etiquette which implicitly defines emotionality as irrational. Most speakers worked actively to preclude the personal and emotional from their presentation in order to speak from an intellectual, systemic standpoint. They were obedient to the "ideal of rational self-mastery" (Lichtman, 1982: 271) which governs behavior in western industrialized capitalist societies. The reason is not trivial: rationality "is the basis of the liberal political demands for equality of opportunity and the right to self-determination" (Weedon, 1987: 80). At the same time, where it enables only certain people and possibilities, "rationality" may be included with other "categories of moral absolutism" as a form of state domination (Corrigan, 1980: 17, 18). This is the ground for much of the contestation between mental health professionals and psychiatric survivors during the legislation consultation. Could survivor issues and their behaviors be deemed "rational" and thereby become broadly discussable as part of an institutional agenda?

Both David Reville and Pat Capponi took up this question in the survivor organizing they did around the consultation. Lyman would understand their work as a struggle over "psychological hegemony." He talks about how dominant groups teach their subordinates codes of behavior such as "reason" or "politeness" which sublimate anger, for example, into nonpolitical forms of action (1981: 67). During the consultation, mental health professionals were tremendously concerned that consumers/survivors participate according to certain rules of etiquette: "Don't give offence. Don't be unpleasant or adversarial. Don't complain or fight. Be nice. Be reasonable. Be considerate. Be cooperative." This behavioral code is an expression of dominant cultural capital. Giroux's remarks about a similar phenomenon in schools resonate:

> Certain linguistic styles, along with the body postures and the social relations they reinforce (lowered voice, disinterested tone, non-tactile interaction) act as identifiable forms of cultural capital that either reveal or betray a (participant's) background. In effect, certain linguistic practices and modes of discourse become privileged by being treated as natural to the gifted, when in fact they are the speech habits of dominant classes and thus serve to perpetuate cultural privilege. (1983: 269)

Where survivors could not or did not comply with the professional behavioral code, there was conflict in the proceedings; people became uncomfortable, upset and/or angry.

Dialogue: Almost a Bit Distressed

Kathryn: Now I am wondering about the public hearing process itself. What struggles or debates are you aware of as that moved around the province?

Professional: Well, at times I felt some of the consumers were a bit too impatient with the Ministry people trying to get the whole thing done. There are **obvious rules** that we all ... **we all have rules**, frameworks that we operate within. I thought at times they were making things very difficult for the Ministry people. Maybe they could have been a little bit more **cooperative, collaborative**, whatever, in terms of **organizing things** rather than "Do it or else" kind of an attitude.

Kathryn: The whole issue of running an endeavor like that....

Professional: Yes.

Kathryn: Organizing it.

Professional: It's a big job for these people and at times I felt kind of sympathetic, almost a bit distressed about what these people, the Ministry people were having to do to meet the demands that were being made of them. Quite frankly I think they did a very good job given how quickly it all seemed to accelerate. That seemed to be an ongoing tension in the process. Are we going to be able to meet the standards consumers are setting for this whole thing?

Kathryn: There was a push there?

Professional: There was a strong push. I just think they could have **taken into consideration** a little bit more about what they were subjecting these Ministry people to.

Kathryn: Do you think that they had a sense of what the Ministry people were having to manage?

Professional: No. I don't think so. That is the one criticism I have. I felt that they were kind of overwhelming.

Kathryn: So, what was it like for you to participate in this process?...

Professional: I felt tense and uncomfortable at times because much of this, as I say, has really been consumers expressing a great deal of dissatisfaction with the system as it exists. I am part of that system. So it is not comfortable.... There have been times when I have felt almost kind of accused.... So that's been uncomfortable....

Dialogue: We Were Yelled At

Professional: I am a convert to trying to look at it through other eyes. I had no problem looking at it through the professionals' eyes. I had a great deal of difficulty looking at it through the eyes of consumers. And I thank the people who helped there.

Kathryn: Tell me how that conversion might have come about.

Professional: Hard work. The willingness to listen. The willingness to try and put yourself in the other person's shoes and it ain't easy. I have been through some pretty difficult times.

Kathryn: That would have been in the public hearings?

Professional: No. No. I am talking about committee meetings. I am talking about dealing with specific survivors which is not the easiest thing in the world to do. But I am not the easiest person in the world to deal with either. I have learned a lot from consumers/survivors. I don't agree with everything they say but they don't agree with everything I say either so one marks off against the other.

Kathryn: It was really coming down to the nuts and bolts of things in committee meetings.

Professional: **We were yelled at.** I remember someone **shouting** from the back of the room: "We are going to make you people hear us. Don't ever forget it. Damn it!" You know? And I went to bed that night and I was very upset. I couldn't sleep in the hotel. Because I said **I did not come to work on these things to be yelled at**.... What I finally said to myself is "You have got to listen to the horror stories in order to know where these people are coming from." And that is sort of the bottom line. And what these people are looking for are those four things that I mentioned to you which is no different than what I am looking for. I am looking for a roof over my head, a job to go to, income, and respect. They aren't any different from me. That has been a two year process. So now I am an advocate on their side.

I did not anticipate the emergence of emotion as a central dynamic of mental health policy-making. My questions were not designed to probe for tension, distress, discomfort and upset. However, my interviews were not tightly circumscribed; there was room for people to bring these aspects of their participation to my attention. Being interviewed gave them a chance to talk about a process which most had experienced as quite contentious. One conversation began with my recognition that the person I was talking to was angry. I simply said: "Tell me about the anger" and the conversation flowed from there. Another person thanked me for the chance to talk about the consultation, the chance to vent some things that were festering.

Participants on all sides of the consultation were left with unresolved feelings but this was particularly true of mental health professionals. They suppressed a tremendous amount during the event — emotions which lingered on for months afterward. They were upset because a significant number of survivor participants did not follow the rules. Indeed, some survivors had another set of rules which they applied to the situation. Consumers/survivors used the public hearings as a forum to express the pain in their lives. Unprepared for this and constrained by the impersonality of their roles, professionals could not do the same; they were relegated to silence.

NOTES

1. The terms of reference for the Legislation Committee are as follows:
   - Provide advice to the Ministry of Health regarding the purpose and scope of community mental health legislation.
   - Assist the Ministry of Health to define and conduct a consultation process with major interest groups.
   - Review input received through the consultations and advise the Ministry of Health on issues and concerns raised.
   - Assist the Ministry of Health to develop draft legislation.
   - Provide advice on other matters as requested by the Steering Committee.
   (Ontario, 1990b: 4–6)

2. The people who talk in chapters six and seven were active in attempting to create community mental health services legislation; to various degrees they were instrumental in what happened. They are also typical of the people currently involved in "consumer participation."
   Mental Health Professionals:
   Ten of my interviewees were employees of the Ontario Ministry of Health. Four were mental health service providers appointed to either the legislation committee or related committees of government. I use the term "mental health professional" to refer to both bureaucrats and service providers. The bureau-

crats I interviewed included five men and five women. All but two have masters level training in social science areas such as social work, criminology, urban planning, psychology, law and political science. Two are nurses with administrative credentials; another is a medical doctor. Interviewees occupied a range of positions including deputy minister, assistant deputy minister, directorships at the branch, program or unit level and analyst/consultant positions. All of them had jobs oriented to health policy and planning. The service providers I interviewed included three men and one woman. One has masters level social science training, one is a nurse with administrative credentials, one is an engineer and one is a psychiatrist. They are primarily concerned with the community sector although in distinctly different ways. One was doing "community" sector work from an institutional base. One is a community-oriented advocate concerned with monitoring patients' rights in psychiatric hospitals, another participated in the legislation consultation process as a "citizen" and the final person was the director of a provincial community mental health organization.

Psychiatric Consumers/Survivors:

Seven of my interviewees were psychiatric consumers/survivors: four men and three women. Their educational status is much more diverse than that of either bureaucrats or service providers. The general picture here is one of disrupted plans and expectations. The group includes one politician and one retired corporate vice-president. These two people enjoy a fairly high quality survivorhood in terms of material stability. One survivor holds a Ph.D.; two have more than one masters degree in the areas of theology and education. However, none of these three are on the employment trajectory suggested by their educational achievements, a situation directly attributable to periods of crisis and disability. Three survivors are on some form of disability pension/insurance. Two have jobs funded by the service system which relate to survivor involvement. These individuals are not affiliated with each other on the basis of paid work or professional expertise. Their connection arises from their self-identification as substantive users of psychiatric services.

CHAPTER 7

Reading the Silences

> I have felt quite threatened at times when the relations and forms
> of knowledge in which I have become competent have been
> challenged. I have found it difficult to confront my own reactions
> and to move forward.
>
> Dehli, *Unsettling Relations*

Corrigan argues that all of us experience social relations and hold certain
ideas which do not accord with the dominant images of society. They
constitute a different knowledge repertoire which he describes as quiet,
implicit and prismatic. "Given a different eliciting context (this different
knowledge) can be vocalized, concretized and, above all, acted upon" (1987:
23). The legislation committee made spaces in which aspects of con-
sumer/survivor knowledge repertoires could be brought forward, spaces in
which mental health professionals were introduced to these repertoires.
These occurrences injected different and frequently oppositional forms of
knowledge into a dominant form. The responses which mental health professionals had to these (delegitimated) survivor knowledge/s can be understood
in part as a variation of "fear of theory" (Simon, 1992).

According to Simon, many students who are presented with unfamiliar
theoretical material in class find this to be "a space provocative of fear"
(1992: 81) which they manifest in silence and/or anger. He relates this fear
to the disruptiveness of theory which "demands an aspect of self-abandon-
ment" (1992: 86) — something I am familiar with not only in the classroom
but also as a feature of involvement with consumers/survivors. "Consumer
participation" elicits silence and anger from mental health professionals;
these emotions arise from survivor disruptions of professional knowledge.[1]

Dialogue: Nothing Valid to Say

Kathryn: Can you say something, you personally, about what it has been like for you to work with this?

Professional: Very frustrating at times. Very rewarding at times.

Kathryn: What is the hardest thing?

Professional: The hardest thing for me personally is **not getting too defensive** which I know I do at times when I feel like I am trying to be supportive, when I think I am doing "the right thing" and **get dumped on.** Or if I have got an opinion that **gets negated.** That it doesn't seem to get discussed through to see whether there is any validity to it. Almost a feeling that if you are not a consumer you can't possibly have anything valid to say. At times that just **pisses me off.** At other times I can understand it. I can understand where it is coming from.... It may be this thing where as grand liberals we decide we know what equity is and we decide to set the parameters for it for other people. Then when the people that are really involved want to say what it is, that our **nose gets out of joint** a bit about it.

Kathryn: There is a notion of equality under this which is a real stumbling block in some way.

Professional: I think that is part of it. And I think the other part of it that is difficult is the **sheer frustration** sometimes of feeling like you are knocking your head against a wall. Not so much lately. I think that is maybe more in the past than it has been in the last year or so. But of feeling that nobody is listening or that the words are being said but that nothing is happening.

Kathryn: Within the bureaucracy?

Professional: Yes. And the role of being in the middle of that. Of trying somehow to still be reinforcing and a support and so on to the consumers, to try to still keep doing some bolstering or encouragement or whatever there and yet still feeling like the frustration with it yourself.

Kathryn: That is a very awkward place to work from, isn't it? To be trying to advance something with one group when ... you are not really "clean" in terms of how you are doing what you are doing with them. So there is no place to stand really that allows you to speak.

Professional: Yes. Sounds like role strain I suppose. But in some ways it is much different because it is a much more kind of ongoing process.

The implications for mental health professionals of taking survivor knowledge(s) seriously include "the potential negation of aspects of one's personal and professional identity and the corresponding investments one has in retaining those identity positions" (Simon, 1992: 86). This is the level at which I was challenged by survivors. This analysis makes professionals' discomfort more explicable; it sheds light on the pain they experienced during the consultation, pain which (like that of becoming "educated") was neither recognized nor worked through.

Dialogue: If We Could Have Had Some Discussions...

Professional: The process of the consultation itself was extremely painful.

Kathryn: Painful to you or painful to watch?

Professional: Both. I thought the committee should have met after each of those sessions, which it didn't do, to process what was coming in. Instead, there were all kinds of incidents that occurred over the organization of the thing during the consultations them-selves that really set the committee members' **teeth on edge**. Everybody got quite **alienated** throughout the process. **Everybody was mad** at everybody.... The only reason things didn't fall apart was because the bureaucracy bent over back-wards to make it happen. If it hadn't I am sure everything would have fallen apart somewhere in the middle. I never would have put up with what the staff put up with. It was just unbelievable. Process and content-wise there was a lot that could have been done. If we could have had some discussions during the process we might have been better off when we set about to write our final report. There was a lot of time being invested by committee members in those consultations. It was also a very emotional experience. **I don't think people wanted to sit down and examine it very closely**. I think they wanted to get some space from it.

Ironically, I had this very same distancing response to the emotional content of my interviews. I found it difficult to allow my interviewee's feelings to enter into the dialogue I was having with them. I kept encounter-ing a belief I thought I had erased: that interviews should be intellectual and impersonal. Once I was conscious of this, a major part of my work as an interviewer became to actively let go of suppressing my own and other people's feelings.

Dialogue: Staying Systemic

Kathryn: I want to talk about the notion of consumer participation that is beginning to run through all of this. You take a very systemic view of what you are participating in here.

Survivor: I do with one part of my brain. The other part of my brain is all touchy feely I assure you.

Kathryn: I think that is unusual in the area. It is difficult for the consumers/survivors that I know and have worked with to have a systemic view of things.

Survivor: Of course it is. I own that problem and I am well aware of that. It is all very well to have a systemic point of view but people are living and dying and despairing and all that junk as we talk. Me included. **I have spoken the way I have because of the questions you asked.**

Kathryn: That is true. I have asked very systemic questions. Maybe I can get at the other part of it. You went to one of the public hearings. I am wondering what kind of response that evoked in you.

Survivor: I think it was marvelous.... I have to believe, whatever the mechanism was, that all the members of the legislation committee were more than touched and gratified by the human experience that they encountered and then became part of. I think it is immensely to their credit that they balanced their processes and proceedings in a way that allowed the humanity to surface without getting in the way of the stuffed shirt presentations that just had to be made in parallel.... The session I was at one of the sheltered home organizations brought 6 or 8 or 10 folks and they were very effective. They were all sitting there. They had come in a mini-bus. They were a real cast of characters. They were shiny clean and sitting there and paying attention and they got to their feet and each one said his or her piece. It was touching, direct, simple and shook the committee.

Mental health professionals struggled in similar ways with the legitimacy of their reactions to consumer participation in the legislation consultation.

They compartmentalized their responses, foregrounding the general and systemic while editing out the specific and personal.

Dialogue: Maintaining the Intellectual

Kathryn: What was it like for you to participate in this?

Professional: Frustrating.

Kathryn: And you don't compare it favorably to other committee processes that you have worked through?

Professional: No. Not particularly.

Kathryn: What were some of the difficulties you encountered in terms of the consumer/survivors representatives here?

Professional: I suppose the basic problem would be that if I expressed a view or voiced a concern that differed, or wasn't understood, or if I tried to bring a different perspective to things there seemed to be a blocking instead of — no, **I am personalizing this too much I think**.

Kathryn: That is interesting though. It is difficult to keep the personal out of this, eh?

Professional: Yes.

Kathryn: Because it has become a personal thing really. I sense that running through all of the interviews. Just how much people have attempted to deal with it in terms of issues but it really did somehow become a personalized process here.

Professional: Interesting. Interesting. I probably would have been self-centered enough to think that I felt that way a lot more than anybody else....

Kathryn: When you think about this process it isn't just intellectual.

Professional: It ain't easy. No. That is right. It is not just intellectual. More than that, even if you think you have got the intellectual part of it sorted out, when you get into the situation and emotions are high about an issue, **it is hard to maintain the intellectual**.... One of my strategies in a committee context which has been I think reasonably successful in the past is to sometimes play the middle role with pulling things and being able to shift it the way I want it to go. It is very manipulative I suppose. But what I found here was that if I did or said anything like that it

> was immediately interpreted as being on the wrong side of
> things and I wasn't allowed to carry it through to the point of
> getting it to where I think it ultimately would have gone.

Editing out the personal is characteristic of professionals confronted with "consumer participation" but it leaves silences around their anger which trouble me. Haug (1992) suggests that silence is a way of coming to terms with something unacceptable. I know from working with the silences in my own speech and writing that they are significant; they generally indicate places in my thought/feeling which require transformation or are in the process of being transformed. Lyman asserts that "silence is as important a text of anger as is vehement speech" (1981: 63). Clearly, professional silence about survivors must be probed.

Silenced professionals are often those who have struggled most deeply to change the(ir) historic relationships with consumers/survivors. The dynamic is generating weariness and bitterness among some of the survivor movement's staunchest allies.

> I think I am going through a very mild form of the (survivor) ritual abuse
> thing. Certainly I am doing a fair amount of wincing and cringing lately as
> the consumers tell me what a patronizing son of a bitch I am. Like you, part
> of me is outraged and part of me is responsive. Most of me is just tired and
> feeling like going out to play in the garden. (Letter from a friend, May 1992)

There is substantial political risk to the consumer/survivor movement here and a challenge as well. Movement participants are faced with the need to facilitate not just the recovery of their own anger but also the collective working through of that anger. Otherwise, the movement may fall prey to what Lyman (1981) refers to as inauthentic political anger. This is anger turned blindly against objectified "evil others" (such as "professionals") rather than understood as a social relation. Doing so unifies the world for the individual but also "mythologizes" it. The history and the nature of the violation which has been sustained are not probed and without such analysis there can be no effective action. Catharsis may be accomplished. Revenge may be accomplished. But injustice and "the power relations which gave birth to anger" remain unaltered (Lyman, 1981: 71).

In Ontario, consumers/survivors are giving themselves public space through local and provincial organizations to debate the recovery (or not) of their anger; professionals are not. Not long ago, I gave a talk in a major psychiatric hospital which put me in the front seat for a small drama. A survivor panel member told the largely professional audience that they had done a rotten miserable job with the mental health system so far and if they didn't smarten up soon they would all be **TOAST!!** Nobody moved. Nobody stood up and contested the statement. Responses to this impropriety in the heart of the institution remained unarticulated, at least within those walls, that public space. Who knows what was said in the small knots of people making their ways to their cars after the event was over, or what was said over a few beers in a bar down the street? These are some of the places where professionals are working out their anger at consumers/survivors for calling them to account. This may provide relief to some individuals. It does not achieve the kind of collective consciousness-raising among mental health professionals which would allow us to come to terms with the challenge which survivors represent. It does not break the reproduction of power which currently characterizes the mental health system.

Emotions were both expressed and managed within the legislative committee and its consultation process. In part, this was accomplished spatially.[2] For example, in the initial hearings which I attended the meeting rooms were set up in ways which were strongly reminiscent of school classrooms, church sanctuaries, and courtrooms across North America. This placed the committee in the teacher/clergy/judge position.

> Thus, in the church, the classroom, and the courtroom, the person controlling and regulating the activity.... has his or her back to the wall. She or he faces those whose participation is being regulated ... facing the door through which "the public" comes. (Phillips, 1986: 229)

I can only speculate about the effect of this on people, although, significantly, room arrangements were one aspect of the consumer/survivor meetings which the committee consciously altered toward the end of the hearings. What is more obvious is the degree to which there were other kinds of constraints, often internalized, on people's ability to express and deal with the feelings they had about the situation they found themselves in.

Dialogue: Keeping Anger Back

Professional: Certainly anger levels have been different at different times.... I was very upset....

Kathryn: Is that one of the rules I wonder? This whole thing about anger and how you express it and whether you make it personal or not when you are doing these kinds of things.

Professional: That's right. Well, as an agenda of government, **keeping anger back** in a very direct way perhaps. You can probably be passive aggressive. But generally when you have somebody who treats you really badly you just have to kind of **sit there and take it**. I don't know what the line is. **You can't say**

"that's not acceptable." So there were different rules for us I felt.

Kathryn: Different rules for different groups....

Professional: Different rules for providers and different rules for consumers/survivors.

Kathryn: So consumers/survivors were given more room to emote?

Professional: **They were allowed** to stomp out of the room. **They were allowed** to tell us that we were assholes — not quite directly. I give some credit. But there was open hostility not only with myself but with a lot of people. **Sometimes it got personal,** sometimes it didn't. It is hard for me to tell. I think that your own ability to handle conflict in some ways becomes projected onto the situation, so I have one perspective. But **we didn't have much of an outlet,** or public outlet. When people were angry **there was really very little that you could do** with it other than for me to talk to other bureaucrats.... But there were occasions when you would have liked to tell people off.

Kathryn: Thinking back on it then how would you describe what it was like for you to be plunged into that?

Professional: I don't know. It was pretty frustrating at times. Worthwhile. Really glad I did it. I am glad it is over in some ways and that we got through the consultations. I think it was really worthwhile. I found it very interesting to challenge my assumptions about things, challenge my comfort level with processes. I found on occasion that I felt uncomfortable and guilty and part of a system. If you work for the government **you have to buy into some sense of due process** — this is the way change gets done. Otherwise we would be on the outside screaming. So you start to wonder. You feel like part of the problem. There is a lot of self-doubt. Am I part of the problem? Am I helping this process along or am I part of the solution? There were days I didn't know.

Kathryn: So it was quite a challenge to your worldview really?

Professional: Yes. And to what extent should, can I adapt to new ways of thinking and try and be responsive and innovative in these areas? I don't know.

Kathryn: "I might have to change my behavior?"

Professional: That's right. I think that bureaucrats all have probably five to seven years of sort of productive life when you are fresh enough out of school before the structure **closes in** on you.

Kathryn: Calcification?

Professional: Exactly. It's been several years. There are limits to the extent to which we can really be energetic. I hope I am still in that phase.

Kathryn: So there are some open spaces that you can feel but the longer you stay with it the harder it is to....

Professional: Well, because the structure is so imposing, **the way that you do things**. You want to be exciting. You want to encourage people and yet you don't know how it is going to get done.

Dialogue: We Don't Have to Put Up With This

Professional: One survivor had been making life very **unpleasant** for everybody. The meetings came to be things that nobody wanted to go to. They were **adversarial**. There were complaints about consumer representation at every available opportunity and many times that weren't available opportunities.... People were at each other's throats. I think the sensitization session may have been seen as giving survivors their due. Maybe it would solve things. Maybe convince survivors that professionals are alright, that we are not all three-headed monsters who have no idea about this.... There was at least one conversion experience.

Kathryn: That's amazing.

Professional: Yes. In the end former enemies became quite jovial. They shared an agenda by the end of the consultations. There were people you just wanted to kill every time they opened their mouths at the consultations about consumer participation. But by the end committee members got the message. A survivor did that basically. Just kept beating on people and saying "Shut your fucking mouth. That is not how you talk." So they got the message in the end. Many of the people who participated felt that they knew it all, that they had been through it before, they knew themselves, they didn't need it, whatever.

Kathryn: I sense from talking to people this real surge around this whole issue. It's like it just suddenly blew into existence and it's on everybody's mind that I talk to. Why do you think that is?

Professional: Yes. Well, in this specific process it is largely because one person was such a pain in the ass, and that we had orders to deal with it. We could just as easily have reached the point fairly early of where somebody said "Look, we don't have to put up with this." I thought of it once or twice and thought "Isn't it interesting that **we have orders** specifically that this is supposed to work?" I don't think that was from any results oriented point of view at all. It was strictly political that you can't let this fall apart. I think if anyone had walked out other than the government people that there would have been.... I am not sure why there would have been repercussions. But the message was clear that we were to continue working together and **we weren't to allow it** to fall apart. It's all coming through from the Minister. This Minister is very strong on consumer participation. It's broad based.

There are tremendous feelings of constraint here, a general pattern of constraint emanating from people who were in relatively instrumental positions. The freedom to express anger, to act on feelings, has been lost, or perhaps more accurately, traded in exchange for the opportunity to attempt to make change happen from inside rather than outside of the system. This is recognized even by some survivors who, while bound in other ways, had a sense of freedom not expressed by professionals.

Survivor: Most of the unwritten rules affect the mental health professionals rather than us survivors. Because you see we are not threatened by the powers that the chair wields or does not wield. We are not threatened in terms of having our jobs in jeopardy. We don't have jobs that are at the mercy of anyone, most of us. We are not threatened because we are a member of any organization and what we think personally is at odds with the organization and the organization holds the purse strings. We have nothing to lose, absolutely nothing to lose and everything to get.

It strikes me that the emotional losses which accompany "buying into due process" are what underlie the tendency I see among professionals to bypass so-called "radical" consumers/survivors and the critique of the current order which their anger expresses. It is viewed as more productive to take up "consumer participation" among the rank and file of "moderate" consumers/survivors who just want to get on with the business of creating their own projects and other types of involvement.[3] Part of me (the prairie conservative?) finds moderation legitimate. I have been in countless meetings where consumers/survivors gave testimonials to psychiatrists, psychiatric hospitals and the treatment they have received from both. I do not want to discount these defenders of the faith, to label them as suffering from false consciousness. It is essential to take people's expressions of their experience as real at some very basic level.[4] However, another part of me knows that there is more going on than meets the eye.

I remember the dynamic which David Reville and I found ourselves embedded in with Users Designing the Future. The group which originated the project was organized by staff from a major psychiatric hospital. Most of its members were uncritical of psychiatry and the treatment they had received while in hospital but as their project developed it took in people who were angry and critical. The first difficulties emerged at the start-up meeting. Some original members felt outnumbered by newcomers and intimidated by angry anti-service system comments which had been made; there was concern that a "hostile" perspective would take root. In response to this fear, David created a structure for the project which was designed to draw in a "broader range" of consumers. It included three progressively larger committees: a steering committee, a core group and an advisory group. The steering committee and the core group met separately each month; the advisory group met quarterly. This arrangement gave the original members a small, regular meeting under conditions in which they were less hesitant to speak; concerns about "hostility" were buffered. What is most striking about this in retrospect is how much energy had to be expended to manage consumer/survivor fears of anger at the mental health system. It resulted in a UDTF selection process which took six months out of a project which lasted only a year. Consumers/survivors know that their anger endangers them: "while members of subordinate groups are expected to be emotional, indeed to have their emotions run their lives, their anger will not be tolerated" (Spelman, 1989: 265).

One of my reference points for understanding the fear of anger is my own experience with it in therapy. When I began I could talk intellectually about my feelings but whenever I was asked to actually be with what I was feeling within any given session I would become either confused or terrified. Asked "What are you feeling right now?" I would inevitably reply "I don't know." For a long time, whenever I did break through into the language of my body what I retrieved was tremendous hurt and tears. As the months went by I realized that my tears were layered over the anger I felt about certain abuses and, more deeply, about the systematic repression of energy and initiative which was built into my female socialization. My therapist encouraged me to act out my anger by bashing away with a tennis racquet on a pile of pillows; she urged me to put words to it, to shout those words. What I experienced in response was a whole series of inner constraints which prevented me from opening into this permission. The most dramatic was finding that at a certain point in attempting to "do anger" my body would simply STOP. I would find myself standing limply with my arms hanging at my side and my head down. I looked and felt defeated. This was a body memory of what happened with my childhood anger. I would express it and be defeated. Over and over and over. Until I gave up trying. Until I could no longer "do anger." Until I no longer remembered that I felt it. Until any rememberings terrified me. In therapy I worked back through this learned suppression.

> From this mourning, one can *get angry*, recover a sense of righteous indig-
> nation and with it a sense of being a self: this in turn opens the way to
> *empowerment*, a sense of the possibility of changing fate; and ultimately,
> *defiance*, political action. (italics in original) (Lyman, 1981: 70)

I know that I am angry. I know what I am angry about. I am beginning to talk about it but I still can't shout. I think about this when I listen to "moderate" consumers/survivors.

There *was* anger among the original members of UDTF. The difficulties were in allowing it to surface. The project had to be made safe enough for people to explore their experiences. Ellsworth's comments about classrooms translate easily to this situation:

> What (participants) say, to whom, in what context, depending on the energy
> they/we have for the struggle on a particular day, is the result of conscious
> and unconscious assessments of the power relations and safety of the situ-
> ation. As I understand it at the moment, what got said — and how — in our
> class was the product of highly complex strategizing for the visibility that
> speech gives without giving up the safety of silence. More than that it was a
> highly complex negotiation of the politics of knowing and being known.
> (1989: 313)

One member of the core group assessed the risks involved in participation as too high and left the project. Her departure was precipitated by an incident in which critical remarks she made to the group about her housing became known to the staff of her housing unit who then made that information the basis for a "therapeutic" intervention.

Another constraint was the demand that we "plan." It took some time before David and I realized that this goal should be abandoned. While members knew much about what existed in the service environment they found it almost impossible to dream about alternatives. This was sharply demonstrated in one session we had about housing. After a thorough discussion of "more and better of what's out there" we asked the group "What about owning your own home?" Reactions were strong and immediate: disbelief, fear, anger. The suppression of members' sense of possibilities was so complete that they censored themselves to stay within the confines of what they had already experienced. Their hopes, their dreams could not be spoken. Regardless of the official permission which this group had to plan their "cadillac" system, regardless of our encouragement to think big, any plan they developed would be constrained by the shape of what already is. I think about this when I listen to "moderate" consumers/survivors.

What I am getting at here is what Lyman (and others) refers to as the "internalization of the master's speech and norms" (1981: 57). Years of psychiatric treatment have taught many consumers/survivors to define themselves in terms which bind them to professional authority; many share professionals' allegiance to the rules of the "game" which was being played on the legislation committee and in the consultation. This is both a feature of their survival and one of the deepest roots of their constraint.

Dialogue: You Need a Professional

Survivor: I think consumer representation is a good thing. It is a good thing to listen to consumers. But it is like an education. When I go to hear a lecture I don't want just a pooling of ignorance with the students. I want input from the professionals. You just don't obliterate the distinction between teacher and pupil. There is a distinction — there are different rules. The teacher is the expert in that field and the students are there to learn. It is like some extreme views in education where you let the student plan the course. You sit around in a pizza party all the time and you wouldn't learn anything. Students don't necessarily know what is good for them either....

Kathryn: I wonder if you were aware of any of the controversies around the legislation consultation.

Survivor: I remember defending the professionals. People say I sound like a mental health worker. But I say that is why I am as well as I am because I was willing to receive help. In other words, part of getting better is the willingness to receive help. And I receive. In my one institutional stay and four hospitalizations I have been given very good treatment.

Kathryn: You talked about that at the sessions?

Survivor: Yes. I talked about that.

Kathryn: How did that go over?

Survivor: I was using the analogy of the teacher and the student. You can listen to the feedback of students but you don't let them take over the class. That is not going to be productive in the long run. You need a professional. And to recognize that difference.... that is part of being a consumer ... that is part of really getting better is to have the humility to receive that help.

Dialogue: The Rule of Common Decency

Kathryn: What I would get out of what you are saying from my point of view is that there is a general tone in the public hearings that it is the survivors who are being insulting, who are breaking some of the rules of procedure. I got a feeling about that just from watching — that there were some rules operating here which survivors break a lot and that causes anger and upset and tension. But what I hear you saying is that there are some other rules which you saw being broken.

Survivor: Well, yes. Again it goes back to your earlier question about the stated rules and the unstated rules. I mean I would call bureaucrat bashing breaking the rule of common decency. Courtesy. Not being mean to people necessarily. Why do you go and be mean to a person? It is just pettiness or something. Or you do it when you are losing, when you are going down. I am not trying to paint myself as some kind of saint. I don't mean that at all. I am the kind of person who dissolves in meanness and resentment the same as the next person does. There is no question of that. I think that is a mistake to put survivors as a class or something like that above service providers. I don't think that is the point. I think that would actually be self-defeating for me and for us as a group. But having said that I think that it is important for us to put ourselves as being different from them. Not above but different.

Consumers/survivors who were not constrained by the implicit and explicit rules operating within the legislation committee were frequently considered to be (at least) "rude." However, they weren't so much rude as operating from a different standard for politeness and reason. As Hochschild points out:

The rebel simply works by different rules of feeling, different standards of truth and falseness of expression, and exemplifies different patterns of aim.

In not feeling as she "should," the rebel reveals what emotional ways we conventionally take for granted.... The emotional rebel who does not feel as she should makes us marvel that rebellion is so rare. (1975: 229)

Where it was articulated within the consultation, "survivor rationality" was a call for concrete practices which would enable consumers/survivors to take up "partnership" roles within a professionally dominated process. The bureaucrats who organized the event learned these practices the hard way.

It is rude and "irrational" to expect partnership from consumers/survivors when meetings are hosted in environments which are not survivor-friendly, on topics which are not survivor-generated, using documents and language which are not survivor-accessible. But the analysis must go deeper than this. Professional governance of the consultation was also accomplished by making "certain topics impolite, certain tones of voice or emotions irrational, or simply defining topics as psychological and not political" (Lyman, 1981: 59). Psychiatric survivors came to the table with tremendous needs; they were required to present those needs in ways which were respectful of professional sensibilities.

Dialogue: Our Guys Are Starving and Dying

Kathryn: How did you discover what the rules were that were operating?

Survivor: Oh, they are the same kind of rules. People have to be polite.... And you can't talk about the past. You have to be very aware of the sensibilities of the professionals sitting at the table.

Kathryn: You are not supposed to offend anybody with past mistakes. And you are supposed to be constructive?

Survivor: In their definition. I have had more lectures about ... "compromise" ... and about "how to represent my people."... At the hearings I couldn't sit. I couldn't. There is a limit to what you can take, right? What I would do so as not to be taken as seriously offensive, like I'm walking out of the room, was to hold my cigarettes up for a few minutes and then obviously be going for a cigarette. "This is not a walk out." So this turkey followed me out and said, "You know it doesn't look good if you are not in there listening to what the professionals say." I said "Well, it wouldn't look good if I spat at the guy either."

Kathryn: Were they lobbying you?

Survivor: Oh fuck. Oh shit, ya.

Kathryn: Over things like what?

Survivor: Oh, anything. Content. Why was I pissed off at this? How people
were taking it. Wasn't it wonderful? There was a continuous lobby
on the part of one person for me to understand another. I didn't pay
attention. I would listen for things that might be important but
when you see somebody's bias and you know that that bias is
absurd, it makes no sense....

Kathryn: What was it like for you to participate in this process?

Survivor: Extremely frustrating. Paranoia inducing. The most simple things
would get so fucked up. Government doesn't operate by efficiency
or reason. And that penchant for looking at the bright side. That's
really quite disgusting. It was hard — first being surrounded by
people I didn't particularly want to be surrounded by. Flying.
Being off balance anyway because there were so many hearings
and so little time. And then exposure to everybody's pain. Our
guys. That was very difficult. And also the conflict on the committee itself as I said where we kept hearing that professionals were
not comfortable, were intimidated.

Kathryn: Was the committee work harder than the hearings?

Survivor: No. Because the public hearings involved travelling. Being in
artificial environments and being in close quarters. Having to
listen to the most obscene kinds of statements by professionals. So
that was hard. The fight on the committee level itself was hard and
frustrating because again it is who are your friends and at what
cost?... But I don't have much sympathy for professional sensibilities. The only thing is you have got to take that into account if
you are going to get anything by them. But it is just so frustrating.
Our guys are starving and dying and these guys have hurt feelings.
It is really hard to swallow....

Kathryn: What are some of the other difficulties that you run up against with
professionals. Besides hurt feelings.

Survivor: Their setting the agenda about what they want to talk about, what
they want to do; being told how best to do what you have got to
do by people who aren't affected.... "Talk about other agencies
but don't talk about mine." And then if you talk too much about
other agencies there is a threat there too. There is also that thing
about support as long as you are doing it to some other body. "It's
great what you are doing out there but don't come back here to do
it." Co-option. Co-optive attempts. People trying to prove how
cool they are. Left wing union people who can't sort of break out

of what they are doing. Left-right wing. Protective instincts are the worst.

Kathryn: Turf protection?

Survivor: Turf and tenure....

Kathryn: So how would you characterize your experience of partnership in the mental health system?

Survivor: Nobody hands it to you. There is none there for the taking.... It is like people come up to you and essentially say "Don't hurt me. I am trying." Not literally but that is the message that comes across. So then you start to feel guilty.

Smith (1992) writes about the male rage generated by women's attempts to displace the dominant male consciousness in university training and research. It taught the women involved that the rules of rational order by which they anticipated changing universities did not apply: rationality as a social order, a regime, has a hidden structure of gender irrationality. Smith understands the rage of male administrators, colleagues and students as:

> a clue to the social organization and relations of a regime of rationality. I take this rage as arising in an irruption of the unfamiliar into the familiar practices of the regime, the disruption of a taken-for-granted ordering of power. (1992: 210)

My reading of the legislation consultation brings me to this place. Smith's analysis suggests that the discomfort and anger which survivors engendered among mental health professionals are not simply individual feelings; they indicate the breaching of a regime. Thus, the regime of rationality is structured along other dimensions besides gender. Within the mental health system it operates to maintain the domination of professional consciousness, a consciousness which is characterized by separation from body and feelings. "Consumer participation" disrupts this taken-for-granted ordering of power with a flood of pent-up emotions. It disrupts the ordering schema of liberal capitalist societies in which psychiatric survivors are designated as "learners," in which they are excluded from consideration as people "whose intentions and choices are the subject of the explicit political and economic theory of liberalism" (Bowles and Gintis, 1987: 17). The situation is deeply contradictory. Having been officially defined and sanctioned as incapacitated through the work of mental health professionals, consumers/survivors are then re/called by those same professionals to act as rational agents within liberal democratic forums such as the public consultation.[5]

The consultation used subtle means to reproduce existing systemic disparities. I am thinking particularly of forms of authority rooted in "symbol, ritual, custom, routine, ways in which things have 'always' been done ... (including) requisite forms of behaviour, attitude, aspiration, feeling" (Corrigan and Sayer, 1985: 193, 195). The work of the legislation committee was profoundly shaped by the imposition of professional routines, customs, feelings and behaviors such as:

> government announcements, committee formation, chairperson selection, political appointments, mandates, terms of reference, proposals, research, documents, public hearings, planning retreats, going for drinks, committee meetings, doing lunch, recommendations, staffing, secondment of personnel, hearing site selection, regional organization of public hearings, expense claims, etc. etc. etc.

The authority of these forms, as well as the expectation that an attitude of collegiality should prevail, was carried into the committee's work within the subjectivities of its participants. It was asserted particularly by mental health professionals when consumer/survivor participation threatened to "unsettle" institutionalized patterns of committee functioning. It was asserted most forcefully when that pattern was broken by behavior which failed to purge emotionality, which failed to recognize and value "rationality." Psychiatric survivors were called upon to bring to the committee subjectivities which supported established forms of order. Those who did not risked being defined as "sectional, selfish, partial, ultimately treasonable" (Corrigan and Sayer, 1985). In the process of their participation, some survivors acquired a political as well as a psychiatric label.

NOTES

1. In this chapter, I use longer chunks of transcripts to interpret "consumer participation" as enacted by the legislation subcommittee. The use of longer verbatim quotes:

   > lets the voices of the people who talked to us be heard more fully than usual with less intervention by us, in long speeches or in conversations, not in short quotes used as evidence for the generalizations we want to make. Long quotes contain more "noise," more material that isn't exactly about the point being made. You can't disguise the speaker's own meaning when you use long quotes. You can't make them say just what you want the audience to hear and no more. In postmodern terms, it deprivileges the analyst. (Schneider, 1991: 303)

2. This discussion about rooms and the use of space is also about discourse. Weedon points out that discourses "inhere in the very physical layout of our institutions, such as in schools, churches, law courts and houses" (1987: 111).

3. I had a long discussion with one of my consumer/survivor interviewees about my use in this section of the term "moderate." He objected first of all to what he perceived as a simplistic categorization of people who have used the mental health system, for example, politically as "radical," "moderate" and, as I have sometimes heard, "tame." He suggested four alternative, interacting categories: 1) by disability; 2) by personal experience with the system; 3) by goals and expectations; and 4) by strategy and tactics. I have no trouble with this critique but do not feel that I need to change my use of language here because of it. I am attempting to bring forward words and categories which I found already in use. My use of the term "moderate" comes out of a discovery that bureaucrats and service providers involved with the Graham Report expected moderation from consumers/survivors. My use of the term does not reflect my own preferences for categorization but rather other people's desire/demand for moderation reflected in the interview transcripts. I certainly grant that this term is confusing (but it is confusing *in use*). As my respondent astutely pointed out, one of the most "radical" of all the survivor leaders, David Reville, used the most "moderate" of channels (legislative procedures, a private member's bill, for example) and voice tones, for that matter, to effect change.

4. I like the way that Lather reframes this issue for teaching practice in schools:

   Rather than dismissing student resistance to feminist classroom practice as false consciousness, I wanted to explore what these resistances had to teach about our own impositional tendencies. The theoretical objective was an understanding of resistance that honored the complexity of the interplay between the empowering and the impositional at work in the liberatory classroom. (1989: 22).

5. Survivors were awkwardly positioned within this struggle:

   In the situations which Kathryn has been studying you have people who have, for a whole variety of circumstances been forced into a situation where their emotions are on display and are part of the agenda for control. Now, in this hearing process, they are being asked to come into a situation which is a complete inversion. The contradictions are profound here for any individual who is involved, directly or indirectly. So that emotions are part of the issue here. And there is a sub-text agenda for the dominant institution. We have got to find a new and more effective way to keep emotions in check. We have got to do that through some participation which these people are going to be involved in. The contradictions are extraordinary. But they are only an extraordinary expression of what we all face in our every day lives. (David Livingstone, Doctoral students' discussion, February 1992)

CHAPTER 8

Returning to 'I'

> Coherence and closure are deep human desires that are presently
> unfashionable. But they are always both frightening and en-
> chantingly desireable.
>
> A.S. Byatt, *Possession*

Eric Peters (1993) has written about gender and race from inside his own
memories of "categorizing moments" as practiced by his parents and grand-
parents. In closing the piece, he talks about his desire to bring it to completion
"properly" and the need to enter into his anxiety about what he had written.
What would his parents think about this unauthorized portrayal? How would
it be received within academic circles? "Maybe I want to rescue myself by
providing some type of interpretive conclusion that will bring the piece
together and demonstrate its significance" (Peters, 1993). I share these
anxieties, this impulse. However, there is no way for me to step back from
what I have written; I have too much pain and hope invested in this text. I
have said things in these pages that I have been unable to say in the past —
about who I am and what I care about. At some level, I am already committed
to working through how these messages will be received.

THE LEGISLATION CONSULTATION REVISITED

The attempt to establish community mental health services legislation in
Ontario began within the mental health bureaucracy. The bureaucracy lost
control of the process during the consultation when it made a brief appearance in the "public" realm. Within that open "moment" the idea of creating
legislation was overtaken by the actual practices of participation; particular

meanings for "consumer participation" were established. A predictable, technical and largely bureaucratic exercise was transformed (to some extent, for a time) into a highly contested debate between and amongst consumers/survivors and mental health professionals over what the issues actually were within the service system. The separations which occurred during this debate, however temporary, reveal ways in which "the state" does not exist (Abrams, 1988). The consultation was an ordering schema but one which was characterized by disorder within the lived experiences of the people involved. The "rational" practices of planning also mobilized emotional investments, desires, disruptions and pain.

Reviewing the literature on governmental inquiries, Ashforth (1990) finds several explanations for their popularity beyond their explicitly stated purposes: education of public(s) opinion; obfuscation and delay; intellectual replenishment of official arguments; creation of social harmony through inquiry participation; political accommodation between powerful interests. All of these he deems partial. He proposes that commissions of inquiry should be seen as:

> symbolic rituals within modern States, theatres of power which do 'make policy' but which do much else besides.... They are part of the process of inventing the idea of the State as a particular form of instrumental rational practice the purpose of which is largely to solve 'problems' in Society. (Ashforth, 1990: 4)

Abrams proposed that sociologists "should abandon the state as a material object of study whether concrete or abstract while continuing to take the idea of the state extremely seriously" (1988: 75). He documents the ways in which the state, viewed as "an entity, agent, function or relation over and above the state-system and the state-idea" has proven an illusive object of study. In contrast, the idea of the state in capitalist societies is highly significant. It acts to conceal "the sort of power politically institutionalised power is ... the actual disunity of political power" (1988: 79).

> The state is the unified symbol of an actual disunity.... Political institutions, especially in the enlarged sense of Miliband's state-system, conspicuously fail to display a unity of practice — just as they constantly discover their inability to function as a more general factor of cohesion. Manifestly, they are divided against one another, volatile and confused. (Abrams, 1988: 79)

The stories of the legislation consultation make a statement about the disunity of order, specifically about the inability of bureaucrats to create cohesion within and through the work of the legislation committee. The stories convey the ambivalence, the contradictory positions and feelings of bureaucrats and other professionals as a challenge to the "basic singularity" (Ashforth, 1990) which is presumed by much of the discourse on the state.

Becoming...

The legislation consultation altered the frame for planning processes within the community mental health system in Ontario. It challenged and shifted the practices of many mental health professionals. But, more significantly for the psychiatric survivor movement, the hearings were a powerful experience within the lived hi(stories) of consumer/survivor participants. Bowles and Gintis contend that:

> action is neither instrumental toward the satisfaction of given wants nor expressive of objective interests, but it is an aspect of the very generation of wants and specification of objective interests. Individuals and groups, accordingly, act not merely to get but to become. (1987: 22)

The legislation consultation allowed psychiatric survivors to create themselves and their interests in ways which had previously not existed. It constituted a temporary channel for psychiatric consumer/survivor "becoming."

Psychiatric consumers/survivors took the work of the legislation committee as an opportunity to create themselves through speaking. Some of this, such as the parable spun by the man with three plaid shirts, was very in-the-moment (see Church and Reville, 1990). Here is what columnist Joey Slinger wrote about the hearing held at Parkdale Activity and Recreation Centre:

> The committee, which itself includes a number of consumers, heard harangues, some quite profane, pleas, funny stories, sad stories — several punctuated by tears, and stories that made no sense to anyone but the teller. For these speakers, even more than for most of us, it is no easy thing to stand before a crowd and express one's thoughts through a microphone, but each tried bravely. (*Toronto Star*, Sunday, September 2, 1990)

Speaking such as this is done not for the sake of debate but for survival, and "Words spoken for survival come already validated in a radically different arena of proof and carry no option or luxury of choice" (Ellsworth, 1989: 302). As chaotic as speaking for survival appears, it is powerfully formative of the people involved.[1] The watchers at these events are also affected: I remember well the catalytic impact of listening to survivors tell their stories throughout the hearing process.

Survivors also created themselves through writing. Some local consumer/survivor groups and the fledgling Ontario Psychiatric Survivors Alliance (OPSA) developed briefs which responded to each item of the consultation paper. The legislation consultation gave them a reason to articulate their views formally and something tangible to articulate their views *against*. OPSA published its brief in the very first issue of OPSAnews (May 1990) thereby circulating a survivor-generated position on the issues to other survivor groups in the province as well as putting it on the legislation committee's agenda. The act of writing briefs and of delegating members to present group/organizational opinions to the committee clearly helped identify these groups *to themselves* as well as to other survivor groups and the mental health bureaucracy. It forced them to grapple with their collective "disbelief" in their own existence.

Judi Chamberlin notes that the American patient liberation movement went through a phase in the 1970s in which members demanded involvement in various professional forums including the President's Commission on Mental Health, and Community Support Program conferences sponsored by the National Institute of Mental Health (NIMH). An unintended benefit of this activity for the movement was that it constituted a funded opportunity for ex-patients to congregate and exchange information (Chamberlin, 1990). The legislation consultation represented a similar opportunity for psychiatric consumers/survivors in Ontario. It inadvertently became a vehicle for survivor organizing as it brought existing survivor leaders into contact with previously isolated survivors and survivor groups. They were then able to identify potential leaders and problematic situations which could become the focus of work within, primarily, OPSA and the Survivor Leadership Facilitation Program. To the best of their abilities, survivors used the legislation consultation as a tool with which to build their provincial movement.

Survivor: I think that the consultation was the most educational thing I have ever had happen to me in my life. I met people. I made friends and I am very happy with that. It opened my eyes in a lot of ways. It helps knowing that other people feel the same things you do.... You are not alone. That's the thing. You are not alone.

Survivor: It was another building block. Serious. Major. The main thing was that so many people came out of the woodwork because of the consultation. We met these new little bunches of people. And we began to follow up those little bunches of people, getting them to talk to each other. So much is going to happen out of that.

The consultation also created a climate within the Community Mental Health Branch of the Ministry of Health which is more supportive of survivor projects.

Professional: I think we have supported the consumer movement in getting profile. I think with the initiatives that are going to happen in the next couple of months we will be able to do more of that. And it will be legitimate and it will be right and there might actually be some support for it.

Since the consultation, consumer/survivor projects have become a higher priority for government funding. In March 1991, the Community Mental Health Branch decided to commit 3.1 million dollars to a special project targeted at consumers/survivors. This decision resulted in the birth of the Consumer/Survivor Development Initiative (CSDI), a program directed by a professional and staffed by survivors. By June 1991, CSDI had funded 42 programs falling within the categories of mutual support, advocacy, economic development, and knowledge/skills production. These projects, located in all areas of the province, created employment for more than three hundred consumers/survivors in the first year. Shortly thereafter, CSDI released a discussion paper which clarified the three basic parts of its policy (CSDI, 1992):

- The Consumer/Survivor Development Initiative does not fund traditional services.
- CSDI supports a province-wide range of independent consumer/survivor controlled initiatives.
- Projects funded through the Consumer/Survivor Development Initiative will have a democratic, membership-driven process in place. Projects must have a board of directors, steering committee, or some other governing structure which reflects their membership.

This philosophy is a real shift away from service provision and professional control of programs. It is accompanied by resources; the Branch has committed another seven million dollars to this initiative over the next two fiscal years. Neither of these developments can be disconnected from the learning which occurred within the mental health bureaucracy as a result of the legislation consultation.

The mental health bureaucracy did not have full control of the legislation committee's work. The bureaucrats who organized the committee were new on the job and found themselves under attack. They were criticized by some members for controlling the committee's work; they were criticized by well-positioned psychiatric survivors for not taking more initiative to facilitate consumer participation. The resulting confusion created more "openings" for consumers/survivors to consult with government than they have ever had. It is moving to see damaged and vulnerable people stand up and express their views in a public forum. It is moving to see them take their place at the board table. But do these developments constitute real power for the psychiatric survivor movement? Perhaps that question can only be answered by coming to terms with the dissipation of the openness which existed in and around the legislation committee. There were distinct limits to its work from the consumer/survivor perspective; the lasting effects of survivor participation are almost all indirect and serendipitous.

Within Limits...

The public hearings sponsored by the legislation committee provided consumers/survivors with the public space in which to speak. What it demanded of them in return was that they overcome all the "invisible" prohibitions against speech which were built into the situation. Survivors were expected to find out about the consultation. They were expected to get themselves on the committee's agenda. They were expected to acquire and decipher the consultation paper. They were expected to prepare an oral or written presentation which addressed the committee's issues. They were expected to transport themselves, sometimes over long distances, to the appropriate regional meeting. They were expected to fund the trip themselves. They were expected to walk into environments of comparative wealth and privilege to meet with well-dressed, well-cared-for, well-educated people. Those who were brought together for the meeting held in a major psychiatric hospital were expected to speak in the presence of hospital staff.

The domination accomplished through such seemingly "normal" expectations is not to be underestimated; many, perhaps most, survivors were eliminated from participation by these constraints. However, something more is at work here. The legislation committee openly invited psychiatric "consumers" to participate in a consultation; most were incapable of taking up the offer. The deepest barrier to their participation was "power within," the internalized disbelief in their own capacities. Lerner describes this phenomenon as "surplus powerlessness," the failure to actualize possibilities which exist because of the deep belief that nothing can change. Both socially constructed and psychological, he traces its emergence through childhood, the family and the organization of work. Rose and Black develop a description with speaks to surplus powerlessness as experienced by "mental patients."

Seeing oneself as sick, having lost the ability to link subjective experience to objective circumstances (decontextualization), and seeing the necessity to perceive quickly the expectations of power holders, the mental patient's potential for independent or interdependent social life in the community is thoroughly compromised. Their social being, or personhood, is overwhelmed by their patienthood; their active participation in and consciousness of historical/social reality is overwhelmed by their passive acquiescence or functional adaptation to and acknowledgement of their own invalid status. (It is) as if their capacity to engage in the process of struggling to live meaningfully has been surgically severed. (1985: 31)

My own associations with surplus powerlessness are linked to gender, to being female. I am thinking again of Smith's (1992) analysis of rage and rationality in which is it men who rage; women observe or are the victims of that rage. Women appear as people who know what they want and are faced primarily with external obstacles to accomplishment. They are not confused, merely beset. This separation is too clean-cut. The most disturbing feature of male rage is when I encounter it within myself as well as in the men around me. I am most hindered in my own liberation by those parts of myself which are invested in male domination. The deepest bond is the agreement, the complicity I feel (often as self-loathing) with male rage. I am beset from without and within. This same dynamic characterized the power relations of the legislation consultation.[2]

Surplus powerlessness acted from within consumer/survivor subjectivities to limit the numbers who participated in the consultation and to shape the contributions of those who did. Seen in this light, the work done by survivor leaders was exceptional. The discomfort which Pat, David and a handful of other survivors aroused in mental health professionals makes the most sense when their anomalous presence is perceived as "an ontological threat to those (professional) identities constituted by the regime" (Smith, 1992: 211). The threat posed by "consumer participation" to the community mental health system is of this order. This analysis is consistent with a Foucauldian view of power as operating through:

consensus rather than coercion, in the form of discursive practices that shape the subjects' thoughts and regulate conduct ... power is not 'out there' in the form of some external identifiable enemy, but internalized through processes of social inscription that shape the way we think — i.e., the landscapes of our subjectivities. (McKenna quoting Rockhill's discussion of Foucault, 1991)

It references in particular that dimension of the state which is powerful in "the way it works within us" (Corrigan and Sayer, 1985: 200). I know this "state" both personally and from the experiences of those who participated in the public hearings.

The Limits of Circumstance

Psychiatric survivors used the consultation to benefit their movement. The consultation also used survivors. Some paid an immediate and very personal price for participation.

> Some of you may know I'm on the legislation committee. You probably don't know I was a casualty of that committee. There was no support built in for consumer/survivors. It wasn't a case of negligence, just poor planning — the hectic schedule, the wide-ranging emotions of the presenters. And so I fell, but I got up again, with a little help from my friends. (Marg Oswin writing in OPSAnews, November 1990)

There was a collective cost in the temporary exhaustion of the survivor leadership and the fact that the consultation turned their attention in directions which they might not otherwise have taken. This seems to be the general character of systemic or organizational change where survivors are concerned. They make gains but not necessarily in the time, place or direction of their choosing. Theirs is the art of rising to circumstance. There are frequently desirable and well-received outcomes from this approach but one is still left wondering what might have been.

The Consumer/Survivor Development Initiative (CSDI) is a case in point. CSDI is both an asset and a liability to the survivor movement. Here is a government initiative partially staffed by survivors which has a progressive policy guiding its distribution of money to survivor projects. At one level, this is difficult to complain about: consumer/survivor groups now have money for projects; some unemployed consumers/survivors now have jobs. The participants are tremendously excited about this. At the same time, through its funding practices, CSDI is shaping the organizational form of survivor activity in Ontario *in particular ways*. Because of its structural location and staffing, these ways are unavoidably (also) professional and bureaucratic. This raises the question of whether progressive policy is sufficient. The answer to this is no at the point where that policy begins to subsume the larger desires and possibilities of the survivor movement — especially where these desires and possibilities have yet to be sensed let alone articulated by survivors. My argument here is in the same vein as that made by Corrigan, Ramsay and Sayer (1980) in their discussion of forms of State domination:

one rallying cry through which modern State forms were established was that of *Improvement* and (less solidly articulated) *Progress*. Who could be against better sanitation, public parks, libraries or galleries, and the wider provision of education? But these were never offered *in vacuo* as 'social goods': they were made available in specific social forms of State provision which, moreover, marginalized and suppressed *pre-existing* class and other alternatives. (italics in original, p. 18)

CSDI contributes to "improvement" and "progress" in the lives of consumers/survivors. In the process, social forms indigenous to the survivor movement, particularly those which challenge existing forms, remain embryonic.

I have pointed out that survivors used the legislation consultation to create themselves in writing. My enthusiasm for this is real but modest. The reason is that survivors were writing into a terrain which was defined for them. In the broadest sense, this resulted from the dominance of psychiatric discourse which precludes certain issues (for example, housing or income) from discussion. More immediately, it resulted from the committee's terms of reference as well as from the content of the consultation document. I haven't forgotten how startled I was when my telephone interviews revealed that consumer groups and professionals working with consumers/survivors blamed themselves for not being able to understand the document. They assumed that the issues were beyond their comprehension. The suggestion that perhaps it was the document which had failed them rather than they who had failed the document was very liberating for several groups. The notion that they could come with their own experience to the public consultation mobilized several groups which had previously felt paralyzed by the thought of being involved.

It was difficult for consumers/survivors to write their way into the legislation consultation on their own terms. They were plagued with the limitations on desire which I observed with "Users Designing The Future" when we asked participants about the possibilities of home ownership. As Chisholm points out, "what we can even imagine, far less who we can reach, is constantly limited by social structures" (quoted in Ellsworth, 1989: 305). Survivors had to match the major operative forms which organize the terrain into which they were moving.

Professional: How did we know how to do that? It's been very *pragmatic*. We've identified *obvious* things that need to be done and brainstormed as a committee about how to do them. Usually it's involved **setting up a small subgroup or task force or working group** to take on these things. The **development of a manual** was overseen by an administrative group of four members. We are preparing another **report** now that we think

> might be necessary. So we have a work group working on that.
> Once we recognize an important issue we tend to put together
> a small group to look at how we can develop an **implementa-
> tion strategy** for it.

These processes were obvious to the mental health professional who described them but they are mysterious to many consumers/survivors. Indeed, they are political issues for the survivor movement in the same category as the announcements, press releases, speeches, letters, terms of reference, briefing notes, recommendations and research reports which led to the legislation consultation. Nevertheless, in order to participate in the consultation, consumers/survivors found themselves preparing "briefs." In order to be selected by CSDI, they find themselves incorporating, learning how to write funding proposals and program descriptions. As survivors acquire these "skills" and take these prescribed shapes, they become coherent to the bureaucracy and the evolving service system. I am reminded here that the title of a conference geared toward implementing the government's current mental health plan was "Fitting the Pieces Together;" one chapter of the conference manual included suggestions for "how to operationalize the concept of consumer participation in planning" (Ontario, 1990b).

Professional: The fact that they are conceptualizing their issues in terms of policy makes it a lot easier for me to relate to. These are real solutions. Consumers are thinking strategically. The same information may have come at me before but it is just **being processed** in a way that **I can understand better now and can respond better as a bureaucrat**. This is a big change. They have changed. It shouldn't have taken that. We should have been able to understand but we have been very good at translating their issues and everyday concerns into policy issues and then developing solutions. The fact that they have moved closer to us is going to make it a whole lot easier. It is sad that this is what it has taken. On the other hand maybe this is what is needed. It is quite exciting.

This begs the question of the lives and the "real solutions" which have been suppressed because the bureaucracy couldn't understand and "process" them as they actually existed.

I have argued that survivors used the consultation as a funded opportunity to organize. What must also be said is that service providers did exactly the same thing using their own channels of communication and influence. Bureaucrats and service providers worked together in spite of their different locations; they had relationships which crossed the more formal barriers of the bureaucracy and influenced the course of particular developments.

Sometimes the arrangements were formalized through the creation of research groups or the secondment of community agency staff; these mechanisms allowed "outsiders" to influence the bureaucracy for significant periods of time. But just as often the collaborative arrangements were informal. Clearly, it was important for service providers to "do lunch" with senior bureaucrats, to be sufficiently compelling to orchestrate such events, and to have the budget (and the panache) to pick up the tab. I haven't forgotten that an important part of my own work as a "national organizer" for the CMHA was to attend to the deals that were going down in the halls or in the bar or over dinner after formal procedures were through. These are political spaces, political times of day and political practices for professionals, the mysteries of which many survivors are only beginning to unravel.

Similar kinds of scenarios are enacted within the survivor movement, however. Take, for example, David Reville's observations about "Users Designing the Future":

> Some important things happened outside the frame of the project. The Official Story does not comment on what happened after the meetings. What is not in the minutes can be as important as what is. I looked forward to the meetings partly because I knew that, afterwards, a select group — Kathryn, a member of the core group, a member of the advisory group and I — would go out for a drink and conversation. The conversation served as a helpful debriefing for me and allowed me — and the others — to gossip about what was "hot" in the consumer/survivor world, in particular, and the mental health field, in general. Perhaps we should expect that even a grass-roots group has elites; maybe we all should have gone for drinks but there would have been issues of income and medication and we didn't tackle those. (Church and Reville, 1991)

While David identifies these post-meeting meetings as a point of separation amongst survivors, he notes elsewhere that it also facilitated my collaboration with Pat. Clearly, then, these informal spaces — interstices — can be used by survivors and professionals to forge and solidify alliances. This is essential given that the formal spaces in which professionals and survivors can collaborate are limited.

In the greater scheme of government operations, the legislation committee was not a very influential body. Its work was limited by a steering committee composed of high level bureaucrats who were chiefly concerned with the "broader interests" of government. A fundamental meaning of this for the legislation committee was that its discussions were subject to organizational problems within other parts of the service delivery system (e.g., long-term care) and, more pertinently, to the need for cost-cutting within health systems generally. Mental health, particularly community mental

health, is not positioned as a big interest of government. It hits the political
agenda primarily as part of the larger picture of health spending.

> I very much doubt whether mental health is even on the political agenda.
> During my five years in the Legislature, there wasn't much debate about
> mental health issues and what debate there was owed as much to the rhythms
> of the legislative agenda as to any consensus that there were issues worth
> discussing.... The most powerful determinants relate to the difficulty the
> government will have in meeting the demands made by health, social serv-
> ices and education. Amid that clamour, mental health has a tiny voice. (Re-
> ville, 1991: 13, 28)

Thus, while the legislation committee was located far enough out from the
center of bureaucratic concern to allow consumers/survivors to enter into its
work, it was perhaps too far out for them to make something substantive out
of what happened. The most direct result of the legislation committee's work,
its much-contested and massaged final report, has not had a visible impact
on government policy and activity.

What then happens to the people who were involved?

The consumers/survivors carry on as best they can. They are rooted in this
struggle whether or not they actually wish to be. It is built into their
subjectivities; they see it in the mirror every morning. For professionals the
situation is different. They can move on. Unless their contact with consum-
ers/survivors is sustained, becomes entrenched, they will "forget" their
"unsettlement" and the affective breakthroughs which the events of the
consultation precipitated.

> **Professional:** My contact is pretty sporadic in terms of frequency and depth
> these days. It dropped off after the committee work ended. I
> don't see consumers all that frequently any more in my every-
> day work.

I have noticed this forgetting in myself. The other day Pat phoned to give me
feedback on my writing. Her comments reminded me of the "correction"
which her reading provides. She pointed out several places where I highlight
the "outrageous" behavior of survivors without drawing out the "outrageous" situation (created by professionals) which they were outraged about.
Listening to her I suddenly realized that she was reading not just what I had
written but also what I had left out. The white spaces: the history of
consumer/survivor pain and abuse within the mental health system. This
double reading is constant practice for her. I have learned a little about it but
without ongoing dialogue the practice slips away from me. The consultation
on community mental health services legislation was like this. It taught
mental health professionals a little about consumers/survivors. But without

a continual process of authentic engagement, we don't "see" them much anymore.

THE RESEARCHER REVISITED

My first reaction was quite simply, "STUN." I was stunned, stupefied, and other similar kinds of non-reaction reactions.... The way in which you have managed to write this, the writing of the history, your history, I found to be inviting, luring, stimulating in the sense that it raised the similar kinds of things in me, made me re-think what I have done, how, why, where, where I am, as well as in the sense that it was somehow forbidden and provocative in its forbiddenness. (Michelynn Lafleche, Survivor of Sociology, writing from Germany, February 1992)

My engagement with psychiatric survivors in research and policy-making has made me sharply aware of the potentially revolutionary character of "consumer participation." The psychiatric survivor movement does not have a strong or unified agenda for structural change. There is considerable disagreement among participants about their goals, and weak organizational mechanisms for mediating these disagreements. However, survivors are agreed upon the desire to speak and be heard, whatever the individually or collectively determined message. Their subjectivities demand that mental health professionals take up the emotional as well as the cognitive aspects of survivor speech/stories. They demand that professionals invest more of their emotional selves in the discussion which they have asked survivors to be part of, and that they allow this discussion to change their work within the system. Although survivors do not talk explicitly in these terms, what they want of mental health professionals are different practices of subjectivity, practices which allow attachment, personal relationship, emotion — even friendship. Moving in this direction would have profound implications for professionals individually as well as for system structure and management. Such a project cannot be done easily, quickly or comfortably. My experience alone suggests that professional deconstruction/reconstruction is an anguished passage in which emotional bending, stretching and (sometimes) breaking is unavoidable.

Rose and Black (1985) argue that the chief task of a mental health worker is to remake severed connections between subjective experience and objective conditions in the lives of "mental patients." It is to contextualize their lives and thus unmake the limited identity that being psychiatrized has created for them. I agree. The difficulty is the degree to which such workers themselves are decontextualized. Right now, we are not making significant subjective/objective connections in our own lives. How can we possibly expect to make them for Others? For mental health activists, then, the formation and reformation of professional subjectivities is a topic of great strategic importance. The most critical task we face is to become connected to the sociality of our own subjectivities, to the ways in which our subjective experiences are filled with and constitute the voices of the mental health system.

This brings me with renewed urgency back to critical autobiography. Mental health professionals need to do critical autobiography. We need to take up Lyman's challenge:

> How can we learn from history? Not from the formal chronicle of events, but from the subjective feelings and thoughts with which we experience the events of our everyday lives. How do we learn from the history that we live? (Lyman, 1981: 55)

I have experimented with writing as a space in which I could learn from my lived history in relation to the lives of consumers/survivors. It has become a vehicle for exploring the exercise of power as a "complex and contradictory process, working at many different levels at once in challenging the historical construction of our subjectivities" (Jackson, 1990: 260). The process of social enquiry is not complete while silence exists around the places where it has rubbed the researcher raw. As Ellsworth says: "I cannot unproblematically bring subjugated knowledges to light when I am not free of my own learned racism, fat oppression, classism, ableism, or sexism" (1989: 307, 308; see also Rockhill, 1987). Nor is "consumer participation" complete while silence exists around the places where it has rubbed mental health professionals raw. These places, once explored, are rich with possibilities for revolutionizing the social relations of professional/survivor relationships and professional presence/s within the community mental health system. My ongoing attempts to do this have yielded insights into the classed and gendered subjectivities which I carry into my work within the service system.

Re/Writing My "Illness"

> But for me, a white and well-fed woman, my place within the market is for now a position of more panic than some others. And from this place within the market (ex)changing me I search and somewhat panicked for what possibly I would have to give you in this time within this place and I find this only: I would give you my dis-ease. For free. (Orr, 1990: 80)

   Not long ago I watched a television program about well-known Canadian author Timothy Findley in which he described how he writes. His partner word-processes Findley's handwritten first draft and then reads it back to him so that they can both hear whether the words have the right cadence. This made me reflect on how "doing readings" has been a big part of my own writing. The other night I read several pages of this work to Ross. In reply, he told me that my writing makes him want to cry *and* that it has been one of the activities which has "saved" us, which has given some clarity and meaning to our frustrated, confused and determined grapplings with my illness over the past year and a half. His words brought to mind Dorothy Smith's suggestion that there might be:

> an inner relation between language and social organization. So that explor-
> ing social organization (or the sociality of subjectivity) involves writing and
> finding out bit by bit in writing how it may be put together, each next
> movement forward starting from the previous arrival. (written comments on
> a term paper, January 1989)

The act of writing my illness has been transformative. It has required me to explore the social organization shaping my experience/s.

   One of the "disbeliefs" I encounter daily is that, after a year and a half of rest and treatment, my body has not completely healed. There is nothing automatic or taken for granted about my movements through each day; they are all carefully negotiated around the pain in my face. I am continually having to adjust my understanding of the depth of my physical crisis and recommit myself to working through the layers of damage which remain. Yet, there has also been significant change. I write these words from inside a different relationship to my body than I had when I wrote my initial illness dialogue. I have not yet worked my way into a state of health which I would call "normal" but I have worked my way out of crisis. I want to talk about the practices which made this change possible because of what they have reveal about "the sociality of subjectivity" and change itself.

   My weeks are structured around three appointments: two with my physician and one with my therapist. The physician is a medical doctor who is also trained in non-allopathic methods including homeopathy. He does not use drugs in his practice. This is crucial to me given that my health crisis was precipitated by antibiotic toxicity. The treatments that I do with him last one to two hours. One of the basic tools of his practice is ozone, a blood purifier. I take two vials of it intravenously each time I see him. This usually takes about 30 minutes depending on how easily my body absorbs it; I control the rate of intake myself. Patience is important since too much, too quickly results in fits of prolonged coughing. Once a week I do an ozone sauna for

30 minutes. This involves sitting and sweating inside a machine which is filled with ozone-laden steam. For the past three months I have also been doing an experimental therapy (life crystals/chondriana) which is intended to bring my inflammation under control and improve the circulation in my face (Merkl, 1992a; 1992b).

Most people that I talk to about "alternative medicine" think of it chiefly as the use of vitamins and "health food." They also think of it as somewhat "weak" in its clinical potency. Certainly this was my preconception. My experience with alternative medicine is just the opposite. Rarely have I done anything which has demanded more "work" of my body. Both types of ozone treatment are very tiring. Depending on the dose, the chondriana elicits a strong bodily reaction which, in my case, lasts for about four hours: fever, chills, headache, nausea. All of this means that for 6 to 8 hours twice a week I am either in treatment or resting to recover from treatment. I have done this week after week for more than a year now.

The most difficult aspect of this for me has been the feeling that, while I am engaged in this process, life is passing me by. People race past with their work, their lunches, their shopping, their families, their holidays. What I do instead is treatment — hours and hours spent alone simply taking in ozone and sweating out toxins. I have never ceased to be impatient with the slow pace at which these activities elicit necessary changes within my body. But at some point I have also become curious about my own impatience. Why am I so afraid to slow down? Why do I have so much difficulty allowing my body the time it needs to get better?

Walking through a bookstore one day last winter I was drawn to a book which pictured on its cover a naked young woman looking at her body in a mirror. Called "Herself Beheld," the book examined the roles played by mirrors in women's self-conceptions as portrayed in English and American novels, poems and short stories. Still in the throes of a problematic relationship with my own "reflection/s," I opened the book at random and read:

> Almost any type of crisis, but particularly a personal loss or even fear of loss, seems to initiate in many female characters a powerful need for literal, as much as mental reflection. When such women look into their mirrors, their psychological condition sometimes finds its visual correlative in at least a momentary inability to recognize themselves. Whatever blow they have suffered thereby becomes the harbinger of a failure of self-representation, a failure to maintain their former equation between identity and ocular presence. (La Belle, 1988: 100)

I immediately recognized this "shock of non-recognition" as a key feature of the complex crisis through which I was passing. I was failing to recognize my own image not "simply" because of physical changes which accompanied a drug reaction but because of much more fundamental changes in how I understood my location as a woman in the world. My illness was a prism. It bent my gaze toward my position within a complex set of social relations, including those which characterize "health care" as it is practiced within advanced capitalist societies. Simultaneously, it forced me to make difficult alterations in my subjective landscape.

I had **doubts** about the route back to health which I had chosen. My body rejected the "medical model" long before my mind did. The decision to enter the realm of alternative medicine was not primarily intellectual. Therefore, I experienced ongoing surprise at being so deep into something so presumably "flakey." The words, the interventions and the entire approach to bodies was markedly different from that which my previous "patient" experience had prepared me to expect and accept. I had no experience with methods of healing which did not rely on the suppression of symptoms, which attempted instead to activate the body's own immune responses. I had no way of "locating" my new healing experiences in a social or conceptual framework which made sense. Even now, having built at least pieces of such a framework and no longer a novice in this territory, I continue to ask myself if I am doing the right thing. To the Western ear, it all sounds so improbable.

My doubts intersect with the **doubts** of people around me. This has been sharpest in my relationship with Ross. Throughout my illness he has been tremendously supportive of anything I wanted to do to change my situation. At the same time, his feelings about my plunge into alternative medicine have been **ambivalent**. While I was in the early stages of treatment it was difficult to tell whether any progress was being made. Ross's chief desire was to eliminate my pain; he did not have access to the sometimes subtle confirmation which I was getting physically from treatment. Whenever I fell into my own doubts, he would **pressure** me to get a second opinion or some other form of treatment. Then I would **fight** back to reassert my original decision. So there was this **tension** between us made doubly difficult by the high cost of the alternative treatment. Since its efficacy is not scientifically established, it is not covered under the Ontario Hospital Insurance Program. I pay the costs of each treatment up front; I am then reimbursed (leisurely) by OHIP for the cost of the office visit only. What this meant in effect was that I was asking Ross as the chief wage-earner to fund a very expensive treatment over a long period of time when it was difficult for either one of us to tell whether it was helping. It has gone on much longer and has involved more **effort** on both of our parts than either one of us could have predicted. The **guilt** which I feel about putting him through this is tremendous.

Similar **tensions** around illness and treatment have built up in other relationships. My mother has been particularly concerned that I am not seeing a "proper" doctor. I have not been able to make her understand that my doctor is indeed trained in the way she thinks he should be (and then some...). She has **pressured** me a number of times to "come home" where I could rest and get some good Alberta air in my lungs. She has based her understanding of my situation not so much on the information I have given her as on her own internalized concept of "good medicine." As a result of encounters such as these with a variety of people, I have become more and more reticent to talk about the treatment I am engaged in. When I do, what I say is often met with **silence** or **suspicion**. I have come to feel a bit like a heroin addict secretly trying to manage my habit.

There have been several points in the past year where I might have given in and gone to a mainstream physician or some sort of "specialist"; in all likelihood I would have been prescribed antiinflammatory medication and painkillers. The reason I didn't give in to the **pressures** I was feeling was because of the work I was doing in therapy. I used that hour each week, among other things, to make the emotional shifts which would allow me to "do alternative medicine." I talked through my doubts and got in touch with my **desires**, separating them as much as possible from the desires I conceived in relationship to other people. My therapist had been through a three year healing process herself and was familiar with what I was facing. She understood the kind of damage which I had sustained and validated my health care decisions. While this built up my personal resources, it also created **tension** as the acceptability of decisions I made in therapy had then to be negotiated within my marriage and other relationships.

I bring this forward to anchor my emphasis on the intimacy of power, on "hegemonic possibility (carried) to the very heart of lived reality" (DiGiacomo, 1988: 114). The power I was subject to in my efforts to shift my body out of established medical treatment was as close as my own feelings. It was alive in the internal voices which conjured up fear, doubt and guilt in response to every change I attempted to make. It was part of my interactions with people who are dear to me, not in the form of demands or ultimatums but in the form of their confusions, their anguish and their labors on my behalf.

I think that there is an important connection to be made here between this notion of power, and illness-precipitated encounters with what Spence calls "shame scenarios." Her own scenario touches many elements of mine:

> Shame of my "ugliness," of my deformed and injured body, of my inability to carry on "being successful," shame of my inability to carry on while I was ill, shame of my poverty, ... shame of my inability to form the perfect relationship, shame of not being the perfect daughter my parents had hoped for, shame of not being the intellectual my tutors had expected. (1991: 26)

When Spence probed these feelings, they proved to be part of a deeper structure of shame related to her class and background. Similarly, my illness and the various "shames" which accompanied it made both class and gender visible to me. Forced to cope with significant and sustained physical limits, I discovered that I live a subjectivity which is poised for flight, specifically, for upward class mobility and "gender escape." Writing about this begins to change it.[3]

Re/Membering Myself

> How did you do it? When did the writing start? Where did it come from? In you I mean? How did the process take place, what did you feel when you wrote, how did you recognise, did you recognise, the writing? And then what happened when you stopped writing, for a day or two days or any length of time? I need to know this from you, for myself. (Michelynn Lafleche, Survivor of Sociology, writing from Germany, February 1992)

My mother was raised on a farm wrestled out of "the bush" five miles from Grande Prairie in northern Alberta. After finishing grade eleven, she went to Vermillion School of Agriculture to study home economics. She met my father there and after a short stint working for Singer Sewing Machines, she married him. Her adult life has been dominated by marriage and children. My life has been dominated by a fierce determination to live out her suppressed possibilities. She is a large part of the reason why I have no children, why I have spent the past 15 years in pursuit of "higher education." My mother is a wonderful seamstress and craftsperson; I can barely sew on a button. Our relationship is characterized by enormous mutual concern and a long history of stilted communication. I remember some years ago trying to explain to her my job as an early childhood psychologist. I told her that I saw mothers, fathers, children and families who came to the agency with a variety of troubles in living together. I told her that we talked about what was going on and tried to decide what to do about it. She listened and was silent. The next day, while we were doing something else, she turned to me abruptly and demanded, "Do you mean to tell me that people actually talk about their problems?"

I remember this sharply because it encapsulated the tension I felt between the route I was attempting even then to chart for myself in contrast with the life of my family. One of the unwritten rules I grew up with was that all our troubles were to stay within the confines of the family. Talking "outside," except perhaps to the pastor of the church, was a betrayal of loyalty. I have been pushing this boundary with them and inside myself for two decades.

The story I have told in these pages is perhaps the ultimate betrayal. I have framed writing myself in as a matter of principle and of method but it was perhaps primarily about survival. Antibiotic poisoning had broken down my physical mobility, my emotional life, my social and work opportunities. I drove the dammed up energy from all of these losses into writing. Large pieces of text were created in the spirit of Barbara Christian's comments: "what I write and how I write is done in order to save my own life. And I mean that literally" (quoted in Ellsworth, 1989: 302). I wrote not in spite of my illness but because of it, not around it but through it. I took up the task in ways which I would never have done had I been "well." I used my illness to crack the familial taboo around personal disclosure. Doing so precipitated my emergence onto the page in unprecedented ways.

I didn't think too much about how my words would be received by my family. My need for self-expression was almost overwhelming; my chief commitment was to getting the words out onto the paper in a kind of verbal/textual cleansing of my intellect and emotions. The day when I would have to confront my parents seemed a long way off; it didn't weigh too heavily on my mind. It does weigh heavily now. As I have worked my way along through each of the preceding chapters the balance of my concerns has shifted from my immediate need to write to consideration of my readers. Recently I found myself going back over the first two chapters and editing out parts which might cause various people pain, then checking myself and reinserting the original words as I reaffirmed my commitment to speaking my particular truths. Still, here and now, I feel less like doing self-disclosure than at any other point in this work. I am seeking protection from the disclosure that I have already done.

One of my strongest "disbeliefs" is that there is a way to save myself and my family from enacting painful demonstrations of the separations which have grown up between us. It's been like this since I left home to go to university, an act which my father referred to as "the first step on the road to Hell."

> I am momentarily back in time staring into my mother's face continually turning back, waving farewell as I returned to college — that experience which first took me away from our town, from family. Departing was as painful then as it is now. Each movement away makes return harder. Each separation intensifies distance both physical and emotional (bell hooks, 1989: 74)

After twenty years of being away, it remains easier for me not to go home than to go and face my feelings about coming and going. I now understand that the emotional intensity of this has to do with its class and gender dimensions. I was leaving/keep leaving not merely flesh and blood loved ones but also the place intended for me within an entire classed, gendered way of life.

> There was no way then that my success could have done anything other than take me out of my class, for to have stayed within it, I would have to reject school and being clever. However, inside that history is a suppressed history which could barely speak itself. The latter repressed and forgotten, is a history of pain and struggle through which I was constituted as a pedagogic subject. What is suppressed is another knowledge which had to be countered as wrong and which I had to learn to abandon. In rejecting this, my mother too had to be rejected and classified as stupid. (Walkerdine, 1986: 6)

For years, one of the ways that I have handled the losses along these dimensions is to diminish my home and family in my own (and other people's) eyes (see Spence, 1990). It's a tempting way to resolve a deep contradiction in my life but one which has its own pattern of tensions. I admire the position which bell hooks takes on this issue even as I feel how far I am from making it a reality.

> Maintaining connections with family and community across class boundaries demands more than just summary recall of where one's roots are, where one comes from. It requires knowing, naming and being ever mindful of those aspects of one's past that have enabled and do enable one's self-development in the present, that sustain and support, that enrich. (hooks, 1989: 79)

I was laughing with friends recently over my urge to have a T-shirt made which features a big prairie rose and the slogan, "My Canada Includes Alberta."[4] It gave such a delicious squeeze to the debate on constitutional reform with which Canadians have been inundated. I was only partly in jest. I have strong feelings about Alberta and my life there. But perhaps I have yet to know, name and become ever-mindful of its enabling, sustaining, enriching features. It occurs to me that this limitation may be a feature of the kind of "amnesia, integration and repression" which Chorney describes as a key feature of urbanization in Canada: "an amnesia which was made more powerful by an urbanism dedicated to forgetting its past" (Chorney, 1981: 557). Stemming the tide of my own forgetting while I live my life in the heart of Toronto is relentless work. I now perceive that it is also intellectual work. Is it possible that my scholarship could re/member my past, that my analysis and my politics might consciously encompass the faces, feelings and knowledge/s of my roots?

"Alice in Wonderland"

In the spring of 1992, I spoke to students taking a third year class in the sociology of education taught by my friend Kate McKenna. She had placed my critical autobiography on their reading list. I stated in my opening comments that I felt somewhat vulnerable because they knew much more about me than I did about them. Even as I said this I acknowledged to myself that much was also left unsaid. The line between public and private in my life has been moved — not dismantled. My critical autobiography took a very particular "cut" through my (previously) "private" life; it was organized around connections with psychiatric survivors, individually and collectively. There were other possibilities for the writing which I did not take up. Specifically, I chose not to write in connections which I perceived between the breakdown/s in my life and the process of doing a doctorate. The most obvious is that my project involved me with people whose experiences of personal trauma and social/economic marginalization are profound; it attended to enormous "internal" as well as "external" dimensions. But beyond this, doing a Ph.D. precipitated an active, suddenly sharp, confrontation with my own surplus powerlessness, my "deep emotional commitment to losing, to being isolated, and to remaining powerless" (Lerner, 1986: i). I understand this now as an encounter with ways I have been taught to be which protect the dominant structures of society (Haug, 1992).

With time out for a brief stint as a teacher, my father spent his working life as a civil servant in the field of agriculture, first at the Lacombe Research Station ("The Farm"), later as a district agriculturalist and finally within the Alberta Agricultural Development Corporation. My mother is a housewife and a seamstress. I have three brothers: a grocer, a welder and a chef. All of them live in or close to Lacombe. Within both my immediate and my extended families, the completion of a Ph.D., particularly by a woman, is unprecedented. Almost from the moment of my acceptance into the program I was engaged in a largely hidden struggle with the conviction that I wouldn't be able to pull this one off. The more things went well and the clearer it became to me that I actually was capable of "doing academia," the deeper the contradiction became. How could I be succeeding when I was a loser? The issue was brought to a head by my comprehensive exam — an abysmal experience from which I emerged feeling that my incompetence had been discovered, that I had been derided and dismissed.

This is another point where I locate the breakdown of my health, one which reverberated against old wounds acquired when I was an employee of the Canadian Mental Health Association:

I experienced my comprehensive exam as another place where what I call the "Alice in Wonderland Syndrome" happens. For example, at the CMHA, they sometimes needed me to be extremely big. I had to do presentations to national committees, commissions and international stuff. They needed me to be large and confident and competent and in control. And I would get that message and I would say "Right, I can. I can do that." And then you would come to something where they needed you to be really small, because there was a problem or something. Or if you were too big you gave them hassle; you forced them to reevaluate their structures or the way they priorized their money. You challenged them and that was bad. That was very bad. And so then what they needed you to do was to be very small. They needed you to be just a beginner: just a beginner, "You know you haven't been here for very long" and "You're just learning" and all this. And I used to think of it as Alice in Wonderland, you know where one pill makes you larger and one pill makes you small.... You never knew how big you were. You needed to check with people all the time. You couldn't trust yourself inside, your own sense of your own being, how much space you wanted to occupy or where you wanted to be. You always had to check with someone else how big you were. And it was bizarre. Again it was crazy-making. (Quoted in McKenna, 1991: 22)

In the past two years there has been a big shift in this dynamic. I have a much clearer sense of what I can do and how much space I can/want to occupy regardless of other people's evaluations. I have encountered my Loser Self countless times in therapy as I have worked and reworked the feelings I have about extended illness. Each time I become more conscious of how to meet the voice that shouts "**I CAN'T**."

One of my favorite books as a child was called "Let's Play Indian." Written in 1950, the story is about a young white girl who wants to be an Indian in the Thanksgiving play at school (Chastain, 1950).

All little boys and girls want to be something special when they grow up.
Betty wants to be a nurse and put bandages on.
Tommy wants to be a fireman and wear a red hat.
Eddie wants to be a policeman and blow a whistle.
But when Susie grows up, she wants to be an Indian!

And the more she is told to sit quietly
And to keep her pinafore clean
And not to step in puddles
The more she wants to be an Indian!

Not a quiet, well-behaved Indian, either. She wants to be a whooping, painted, war-dancing Indian with beads and feathers and tomahawks!

The story goes on to describe how Susie is forced to play the leading lady Pilgrim because she has long blonde hair. No amount of good behavior will sway her teacher from this decision. It is only by chance, when the boy who was to play Big Chief Wopahasee gets the mumps that Susie is allowed to take his place.

> She was so happy she could hardly breathe. When it came time for her to walk on the stage and make Big Chief Wopahassee's solemn speech, she was so excited that she forgot all about the speech. She just ran out on the stage, whooping and yelling and waving her tomahawk. Then she went into a war dance and stomped all around the Pilgrims. The faster she danced, the louder she whooped until she sounded like a tribe of Indians on the warpath!!
>
> When Ellen, Harold, Bill and Lucy saw Susie having so much fun, they joined in and they all danced around the stage, screaming and whooping, beating their tom-toms and waving their tomahawks!
>
> Miss Dillingway thought she would faint! She pulled the curtains together quickly. Then she heard all the mothers and fathers roaring with laughter and clapping their hands as hard as they could. "Well!" said Miss Dillingway. "Well! All I have to say is that our next play will be a Christmas play. There will be no Indians in that!"
>
> But Susie didn't care. She was happy! For five whole minutes she had been a really truly Indian!

My heart was with Susie. All through my childhood I struggled with being "the only girl" in the family, with the limitations I felt from that position on "whooping it up" like my brothers. I see now the complex and hierarchical ways in which "Let's Play Indian" (including the accompanying pictures) constructs race, gender, class and other dimensions of difference. I also see how it validates rationality. Here we have a girl who is unhappy with her part in the social order. She craves the mess and chaos of emotionality, a quality which is considered so alien that it is ascribed to "Indians." When she does get a chance to try it on it she forgets her "speech." Emotions take her over. And the other children as well. The parents laugh but the teacher knows better. This is dangerous. This was a one time event. There will be no more "Indians."

I remember this in connection with my struggles to incorporate the personal into my doctoral work. I was certain that my inclusion of the subjective would be rejected, that I would have to absorb some punishment for bringing it forward. While working my fears through with David Livingstone, my supervisor, I realized that he was not a person to me. Rather, he symbolized a particular type of scholarship which was white, male, established, theoretical, rational. Our conversations consistently had a shock element for me as I confronted the dysjuncture between the things that he symbolized and how he actually responded to my work. Slowly, I worked out with him deeply ingrained patterns of (female) response to (male) authority in education. I confronted my disbelief that I can make a place for myself "in the ordered halls of academe" as a woman who speaks from her (emotional) voice/s (Rockhill, 1987). Are there possibilities within academia for my future which were not there previously?

Envisioning Possible Future/s

> Last week in a non-credit course on illness that I teach to senior citizens I was discussing a quotation from May Sarton, whom I don't like in some ways, but who also gets some things just right. She either told a friend or was told, "You have been to hell and back and you have not realized that this creates a responsibility." You, on the other hand, realize exactly that it creates a responsibility, but you seem to be seeking the venue in which to exercise that responsibility. This is very difficult.
>
> *(Letter from Arthur Frank, February 1992)*

All the way through my doctorate, I struggled with fantasies about how academic work should look and sound. David Livingstone gave me much-needed affirmation and encouragement. "But," I asked him, "Is it sociology?" "I don't know," he replied. "I don't care (right now ... keep writing)." At the conclusion of my dissertation I was more anxious than ever about whether it displayed "constitutional aspects ... of sociological discourse" (Smith, 1991: 165), with whether I had "written like a man" (Schneider, 1991: 298). Part of me secretly hoped that I had learned how to write so that other people recognized me as "doing sociology." Other parts of me were/are determined that I not betray my desire to break out of objectified modes of thinking and writing. This debate is part of the larger question of my possible future/s. Its resolution will depend at least in part on the kind of work that I am able to find/create for myself in the future. As Arthur Frank points out, I am looking for a venue in which to exercise the responsibility created by my journey over the past few years.

In his history of Ontario's mental health system, Harvey Simmons concluded that "as we enter the 1990s ... the days of elite policymaking in mental health are past"; psychiatric authority has diminished and there are now many pressure groups determined to influence government policymaking in their interests" (1989: 267). In reviewing his book, I conceded the reality of this general trend but argued that Simmons had overestimated the extent of the shift.

> Policymaking has been democratized primarily among the professional/managerial groups: "the elite" is now more broadly representative of those who work in the field. Rather significantly, the users of the mental health system are virtually untouched by this process. The long history of their exclusion continues. (Church, 1992b: 39)

Since I wrote these words the situation has shifted again. I see a community mental health system which is undergoing significant change around the question of who is to be involved in decision-making at local, regional and provincial levels of organization. In the past two years, it has become "politically incorrect" for these processes to occur without the presence of psychiatric consumers/survivors. The debate is over who those survivors will be, how many there will be, and what, if any, the new rules of the game will be.

Many mental health professionals have become uncertain about how to work in this new climate. They are confused and often angry about the changes going on around them but rarely discuss these feelings publicly. There is an urgent need for their silence to be broken before it builds into a backlash which swamps the inroads which consumers/survivors are beginning to make. I want to engage with this problem. I see the need to develop specific practices which would enable consumers/survivors and mental health professionals to work together across difference (Narayan, 1988). I see the need to develop practices which would shift mental health professionals into alignment with survivors rather than the other way around. I want to attempt these tasks with hope, acknowledging "more openness in a situation than the situation easily reveals" and acting "in the present as if an alternative had already begun to emerge" (Simon, 1992, 3). My strongest sense of where to begin is with my own words. I would like to continue to write across the boundaries between psychiatric consumers/survivors and mental health professionals, to make the "resistant discourses" (Weedon, 1987: 174) of the mental health field available to survivors. I would like to see whether the deeply held values and commitments which have given this work its shape and character can flourish in other institutions. This project has hardly begun. Indeed, it has taken me all this time simply to formulate it.

INVOKING CLOSURE

The other day I was sitting in a meeting with a group comprised of mental health professionals and psychiatric consumers/survivors, one of whom was Pat Capponi. In the middle of making a point, Pat began to use the word "discourse" in a sentence. She caught herself after the first syllable, rolled her eyes at me from under her big black hat and carefully chose another word. Thinking back over all the times that she has forced me to abandon my academic verbiage as inappropriate for our joint project, I felt a certain amount of glee that a word or two had captured her unconscious. At the same time the incident set off a warning signal in my mind. I have learned the importance of survivor speech. I do not want psychiatric survivors to lose their capacity for it as a result of "consumer participation." I have come to value their ability to make me uncomfortable.

My critical autobiography challenges academic forms in the same ways that survivor narratives challenge service system forms. It brings to these pages the emotive qualities of survivor speaking out, and, perhaps, instills in my readers the same kind of discomfort felt by mental health professionals who sat through the provincial legislation consultation. The service providers and bureaucrats I talked to openly expressed discomfort with survivor speech. This is an indication of how professionals have been taught to monitor and regulate themselves. Events such as the consultation attempt to "make" survivor subjectivities along similar "rational" lines. In these ways the hegemonic forms and relations of the mental health system are reproduced. Ironically, the educational activities and forms which facilitate my making this analysis also "make" my subjectivity in keeping with the same pattern. The knowledge construction practices in which survivors become embedded through "consumer participation" are of the same order as those which I engage in to do research. Perceiving this, I have come to understand that a critical part of doing activist research is to generate discomfort, to exercise survivor voice/s.

For ten years my life has been intricately linked to psychiatric survivors. It has been a time of profound upheaval for me — professionally, politically and personally. Of particular significance is the powerful conjunction which emerged between my penetration into the lives of psychiatric survivors and my plunge into sustained encounters with the fragility of my own physical and emotional health. The most compelling insight I derive from this "unsettlement" is that it reflects the shake-up which is occurring more generally among mental health professionals faced with "consumer participation." This in turn mirrors the loss of coherence inherent in policy-making. Ultimately, self-reflection has revealed undeniable connections between reformation of identities and reformation of policies, between subjectivities and large scale social relations.

NOTES

1. For example, it was at a public meeting about "crazies" in Parkdale which precipitated Pat Capponi's transition into activism:

    I was getting angrier and angrier, and fighting with myself to keep quiet. It was hard. I kept thinking about Alice and Gary and Haddie, what they went through every day, and how humiliated they'd be to hear all this. I stood up, the same way I had at college meetings, looking more assured than I felt, and I tried to conceal my shaking. The individual chairing the meeting recognized me before I had any clear idea what I was going to say. I'd be damned if I'd let them know I was intimidated, so I cleared my throat and just let the words come.... (B)efore the meeting ended I had figured out what I could do about the boarding house and the people in it. How I might try to change things. (Capponi, 1992: 195, 196).

2. In a recent debate over "schooling," Ellsworth (1989) argues that Henry Giroux's "formula for dialogue requires and assumes a classroom of participants united on the side of the subordinated against the subordinators, sharing and trusting in an 'us-ness' against 'them-ness.' This formula fails to confront dynamics of subordination present among classroom participants and within classroom participants in the form of multiple and contradictory subject positions" (1989: 315). The argument I am making about professionals and survivors in the mental health system takes this same line. The psychiatric survivor movement is not characterized by that quality of one-ness in which all participants understand themselves to be oppressed. They don't necessarily experience the dynamic of their relationships to professionals as an "us" and a "them." This is one of the basic difficulties in creating and sustaining a survivor movement.

3. I am thinking here of Haug's (1992) comments:

    Simply to write up experiences and memories changes a good deal. It is necessary to make a selection, to set priorities, choose a suitable vocabulary, distance oneself appropriately, uncover similarities, posit a reader and hence fill in necessary details and make connections between events and so on. Above all it is vital to make conscious what has been experienced, just as if it had already been made conscious before. That doesn't just require effort, it also calls for a quite different view of things, and, conversely, you suddenly discover in the course of writing all sorts of things that you hadn't realized, all sorts of things that you wanted to say and which now press on you. In short, writing is a form of production, an activity which creates a new consciousness.

4. During the country's most recent constitutional debate (can Canada accommodate the aspirations of primarily French-speaking Quebec?) federalist supporters came up with the slogan "My Canada includes Quebec." It stirred mixed feelings in me. I voted 'yes' in the referendum but the invisibility of Western alienation in the debate (an outgrowth of the West's long history of exploitation by central Canada) really rankled. I've paraphrased the federalism/separatism slogan; American readers would understand these relations in a state rights context.

Bibliography

Abrams, P. (1988). Notes on the difficulty of studying the state. *Journal of Historical Sociology*, 1(1), 58–89.

Alcoff, L., and Gray, L. (1993). Survivor discourse: transgression or recuperation? *Signs*, Winter, 260–290.

Ashforth, A. (1990). Reckoning schemes of legitimation: on commissions of inquiry as power/knowledge forms. *Journal of Historical Sociology*, 3(1), 1–22.

Ashmore, M. (1989). *The Reflexive Thesis: Wrighting Sociology of Scientific Knowledge*. Chicago: University of Chicago Press.

Bakhtin, M. (1981/86). *The Dialogic Imagination*. Holquist, M., ed. Austin: University of Texas Press.

Ball, S. (1990). *Politics and Policy-Making in Education: Explorations in Policy Sociology*. London: Routledge.

Bannerji, H., Carty, L., Dehli, K., Heald, S., and McKenna, K. (1991). *Unsettling Relations: The University as a Site of Feminist Struggles*. Toronto: Women's Press.

Barker, I., and Peck, E., eds. (1987). *Power in Strange Places: User Empowerment in Mental Health Services*. London, England: Good Practices in Mental Health.

Becker, H., ed. (1964). *The Other Side — Perspectives on Deviance*. Glencoe, IL: Free Press.

Becker, H., McCall, M., Morris, L., and Meshejian, P. (1989). Theatres and communities: three scenes. *Social Problems*, 36(2), 93–116.

Benston, M. (1987). Feminism and systems design. A paper presented at "The Effects of Feminist Approaches on Research Methodologies" Conference, Calgary.

Blanch, A.K. (1985). *Community Mental Health Ideology and Administration of State Mental Health Services: Changes in State Mental Health Agencies from 1960 to 1984.* Unpublished doctoral dissertation, University of Vermont, Burlington.

Bowles, S., and Gintis, H. (1987). *Democracy and Capitalism: Property, Community and the Contradictions of Modern Social Thought.* New York: Basic Books.

Britzman, D. (1989). *The Terrible Problem of 'Knowing Thyself': Toward a Poststructural Account of Teacher Identity.* A paper presented to The Ethnography and Education Research Forum, University of Pennsylvania.

Burstow, B., and Weitz, D., eds. (1988). *Shrink Resistant: The Struggle Against Psychiatry in Canada.* Vancouver: New Star Books.

Byatt, A.S. (1990). *Possession: A Romance.* London: Vintage.

Capponi, P. (1992). *Upstairs in the Crazy House: The Life of a Psychiatric Survivor.* Toronto: Viking.

Chamberlin, J. (1978). *On Our Own: Patient-Controlled Alternatives to the Mental Health System.* New York: McGraw-Hill.

Chamberlin, J. (1990). The ex-patients' movement: where we've been and where we're going. *The Journal of Mind and Behavior*, 11(3/4), 323–336.

Chastain, M.L. (1950). *Let's Play Indian.* New York: Wonder Books.

Chorney, H. (1981). Amnesia, integration and repression: the roots of Canadian urban political culture. In Dear, M., and Scott, A.J., eds. *Urbanisation and Urban Planning in Capitalist Society.* London: Methuen.

Church, K. (1986). *From Consumer to Citizen.* Toronto: Canadian Mental Health Association (National).

Church, K. (1991a). *Whittling Away at the Paradigm: Systemic and Non-Instructed Advocacy.* Toronto: Psychiatric Patient Advocate Office.

Church, K. (1991b). I went to the doctor. *Canadian Family Physician*, 37, 302–309.

Church, K. (1992a). Book reviews: Unbalanced: mental health policy in Ontario, 1930–1989. *Canada's Mental Health*, 40(1), 39.

Church, K. (1992b). *Moving Over: A Commentary on Power-Sharing.* Toronto: Psychiatric Survivor Leadership Facilitation Program.

Church, K., and Capponi, P. (1991). *Re/Membering Ourselves: A Resource Book on Psychiatric Survivor Leadership Facilitation.* Toronto: Psychiatric Survivor Leadership Facilitation Program.

Church, K., and Pakula, A. (1983). *Employment Opportunities for People Labelled as Psychiatrically Disabled.* Toronto: Canadian Mental Health Association (National).

Church, K., and Reville, D. (1988). *User Involvement in Mental Health Services in Canada: A Work in Progess.* Paper presented to an international converence on user involvement, University of Sussex, England.

Church, K., and Reville, D. (1989). User involvement in the mental health field in Canada. *Canada's Mental Health,* 37(2), 22–25.

Church, K., and Reville, D. (1990). Do the right thing* right. *Canadian Review of Social Policy,* 26, 77–81.

Church, K., and Reville, D. (1991). *"Users Designing the Future": Demystifying the Politics of Psychiatric Consumer/Survivor Participation.* A paper developed for the Secretary of State of Canada. Available from David Reville, Queen's Park, Toronto.

Cohen, L. Take this waltz. *I'm Your Man.* Columbia Records.

Consumer/Survivor Development Initiative (April, 1992). *Policy Discussion Paper.* Available from CSDI, 2160 Yonge Street, 3rd Floor, Toronto, M4S 2Z3.

Corrigan, P. (1987). In/forming schooling. In Livingstone, D., ed. *Critical Pedagogy and Cultural Power.* South Hadley, Mass: Bergin and Garvey.

Corrigan, P., Ramsay, H., and Sayer, D. (1980). The state as a relation of production. In Corrigan, P., ed. *Capitalism, State Formation and Marxist Theory.* London: Quartet Books.

Corrigan, P., and Sayer, D. (1985). *The Great Arch: English State Formation as Cultural Revolution.* Oxford: Basil Blackwell.

Crozier, L. (1988). *Angels of Flesh, Angels of Silence.* Toronto: McClelland and Stewart.

Cully, M., and Portuges, C., eds. (1985). *The Dynamics of Feminist Teaching.* Boston: Routledge and Kegan Paul.

Czukar, G. (1988). *Legislative Implications of Changing Mental Health Policy.* Toronto: Canadian Mental Health Association (National).

Dain, N. (1989). Critics and dissenters: reflections on "anti-psychiatry" in the United States. *Journal of the History of the Behavioral Sciences,* 25 (January), 3–24.

Dehli, K. (1991). Leaving the comfort of home: working through feminisms. In *Unsettling Relations: The University as a Site of Feminist Struggles.* Toronto: Women's Press.

DiGiacomo, S. (1987). Biomedicine as a cultural system: an anthropologist in the kingdom of the sick. In Baer, H., ed. *Encounters with Biomedicine: Case Studies in Medical Anthropology*. New York: Gordon and Breach Science Publishers.

DiGiacomo, S. (1988). Metaphor as illness: postmodern dilemmas in the representation of body, mind and disorder. *Medical Anthropology*, 14, 109–137.

Doyal, L. (1979). *The Political Economy of Health*. London: Pluto Press.

Elling, R. (1986). *The Struggle for Workers' Health: A Study of Six Industrialized Countries*. Farmingdale, NY: Baywood Publishing Co.

Ellsworth, E. (1989). Why doesn't this feel empowering? working through the repressive myths of critical pedagogy. *Harvard Educational Review*, 59(3), 297–324.

Estroff, S. (1981). *Making It Crazy: An Ethnography of Psychiatric Clients in an American Community*. Berkeley: University of California Press.

Foucault, M. (1981). Questions of method: an interview with Michel Foucault. *Ideology and consciousness*, 8, 3–14.

Frank. A. (1990). Bringing bodies back in: a decade in review. In Featherstone, M., ed. *Theory, Culture and Society: Explorations in Critical Social Science*, 7, 131–162.

Frank, A. (1991). *At the Will of the Body: Reflections on Illness*. Boston: Houghton Mifflin.

Fraser, R. (1984). *In Search of a Past*. London: Verso.

Gazzola, P. (1987). Community as a way of life — the next step forward. *Just Cause*, 5(2), 9–11.

Geertz, C. (1988). *Works and Lives: The Anthropologist as Author*. Stanford, CA: Stanford University Press.

Gendler, R. (1984). *The Book of Qualities*. New York: Harper and Row.

Giddens, A. (1984). *The Constitution of Society: Outline of the Theory of Structuration*. Berkely: University of California Press.

Giroux, H. (1983). Theories of reproduction and resistance in the new sociology of education: a critical analysis. *Harvard Educational Review*, 53(3), 257–293.

Gold, N. (1988). Mental health in Canada 1947–1957. *Canadian Social Work Review*, 5, 206–223.

Goldberg, N. (1986). *Writing Down the Bones: Freeing the Writer Within*. Boston: Shambhala Publications.

Goldberg, N. (1990). *Wild Mind: Living the Writer's Life*. New York: Bantam.

Grieg, N. (1987). Codes of conduct. In Hanscrombe, G., and Humphries, M., eds. *Heterosexuality*. London: GMP Publishers.

Griffin, J. (1989). *In Search of Sanity: A Chronicle of the Canadian Mental Health Association 1918–1988*. London: Third Eye.

Hale, S. (1992). Facticity and dogma in introductory sociology texts: the need for alternative methods. In Carroll, W., Christiansen-Ruffman, L., Currie, R., and Harrison, D., eds. *Fragile Truths: Twenty-Five Years of Sociology and Anthropology in Canada*. Ottawa: Carleton University Press.

Hanh, Thich Nhat (1988). *The Sun My Heart: From Mindfulness to Insight Contemplation*. Berkeley, CA: Parallax Press.

Hansen, P., and Muszynski, A. (1990). Crisis in rural life and crisis in thinking: directions for critical research. *Canadian Review of Sociology and Anthropology*, 27(1), 1–22.

Haug, F. (1992). *Beyond Female Masochism: Memory-Work and Politics*. London: Verso.

Hearn, J. (1983). *Birth and Afterbirth: A Materialist Account*. Achilles Heel Publications.

Heilbrun. C. (1988). *Writing a Woman's Life*. New York: Norton.

Henriques, J., Hollway, W., Urwin, C., Venn, C., and Walkerdine, V. (1984). *Changing the Subject: Psychology, Social Regulation and Subjectivity*. London: Methuen.

Hochschild, A. (1975). The sociology of feeling and emotion: selected possibilities. In Millman, M., and Kaplan, R., eds. *Another Voice*. New York: Anchor Books.

hooks, b. (1989). *Talking Back: Thinking Feminist, Thinking Black*. Boston: South End.

Hutcheon, L. (1988). A postmodern problematics. In Merrill, R., ed. *Ethics/Aesthetics: Post-Modern Positions*. Washington, DC: Maisonneuve Press.

Jackson, D. (1990). *Unmasking Masculinity: A Critical Autobiography*. London: Unwin Hyman.

Johnson, B. (1987). *A World of Difference*. Baltimore: Johns Hopkins University Press.

Kabat-Zinn, J. (1990). *Full Catastrophe Living: Using the Wisdom of Your Body and Mind to Face Stress, Pain and Illness*. New York: Delta.

Kelman, S. (1975). The social nature of the definition problem in health. *International Journal of Health Services*, 5, 625–624.

Killian, L., and Bloomberg, S. (1975). Rebirth in a therapeutic community: a case study. *Psychiatry*, 38(1), 39–54.

Kleinman, A. (1988). *The Illness Narratives: Suffering, Healing, and the Human Condition*. New York: Basic Books.

La Belle, J. (1988). *Herself Beheld: The Literature of the Looking Glass*. Ithaca, New York: Cornell University Press.

Lafleche, M. (1990). Unpublished notes for Survivors of Sociology.

Lather, P. (1989). *Deconstructing/Deconstructive Inquiry: Issues in Feminist Research Methodologies*. A paper presented at the New Zealand Women's Studies Association Conference.

Lather, P. (1991). *Getting Smart: Feminist Research and Pedagogy with/in the Postmodern*. New York: Routledge.

Lennon, M., Link, B., Marbach, J., and Dohrenwend, B. (1989). The stigma of chronic facial pain and its impact on social relationships. *Social Problems*, 36(2), 117–134.

Lerner, M. (1986). *Surplus Powerlessness: The Psychodynamics of Everyday Life ... and the Psychology of Individual and Social Transformation*. Oakland, CA: The Institute for Labor and Mental Health.

Lichtman, R. (1982). *The Production of Desire: The Integration of Psychoanalysis into Marxist Theory*. New York: The Free Press.

Lightman, E. (1992). *A Community of Interests: The Report of the Commission of Inquiry into Unregulated Residential Accommodation*. Toronto: Queen's Printer for Ontario.

Lord, J. (1984). *Consumer Self-Help Groups in Canada: Preliminary Issues and Analysis*. Toronto: Canadian Mental Health Association (National).

Lordes, A. (1984). *Sister Outsider*. New York: The Crossing Press.

Lovett, L. If I had a boat. *Pontiac*. MCA Records.

Lugones, M and Spelman, E. (1983). Have we got a theory for you! feminist theory, cultural imperialism, and the demand for 'the women's voice.' *Women's Studies International Forum*, 573–581.

Lyman, P. (1981). The politics of anger: on silence, ressentiment and political speech. *Socialist Review*, 57, Vol. 11(3), 55–74.

Mairs, N. (1986). *Plaintext: Deciphering a Woman's Life*. Tuscon: University of Arizona Press.

Mairs, N. (1989). *Remembering the Bone House — An Erotics of Place and Space*. New York: Harper and Row.

Marcus, G., and Fischer, M. (1986). *Anthropology as Cultural Critique: An Experimental Moment in the Human Sciences*. Chicago: University of Chicago Press.

McKenna, K. (1990). *Learning to Talk About It: The Politics of Re/Membering*. Unpublished paper.

McKenna, K. (1991). *Com(e) (A)part Mentalizations: Forming Academic Subject(ivities)*. Unpublished master's thesis, University of Toronto.

McKnight, J. (1986). Regenerating community. In Church, K., ed. *From Consumer to Citizen*. Toronto: Canadian Mental Health Association (National).

Merkl, G. (1992a). The origin of life: life crystal and the chondriana. *Consumer Health Newsletter*, 15(4).

Merkl, G. (1992b). A new treatment for cancer and degenerative disease: the chondriana. *Consumer Health Newsletter*, 15(5).

Mills, C. (1957). *The Sociological Imagination*. London: Oxford University Press.

Millett, K. (1990). *The Loony-Bin Trip*. New York: Simon and Schuster.

Morwood, G. (1984). The role of a national voluntary organization: The Canadian Mental Health Association (CMHA). In Lumsden, D., ed. *Community Mental Health Action: Primary Prevention Programming in Canada*. Ottawa: Canadian Public Health Association.

Murphy, R. (1987). *The Body Silent*. New York: Holt.

Narayan, U. (1988). Working together across difference: some considerations on emotions and political practice. *Hypatia*, 3(2), 31–47.

National Network for Mental Health. (1990). *Without Restraint*, Spring 2(1).

National Network for Mental Health. (1990). *Without Restraint*, Summer, 2(2).

National Network for Mental Health. (1990–91). *Without Restraint*, Fall/Winter, 2(3).

National Network for Mental Health. (1990). *Without Restraint*, Spring/Summer, 3(1).

National Network for Mental Health. (1992). *Without Restraint*, Fall, 3(2).

Nelson, C. (1986). *Theory in the Classroom*. Chicago: University of Illinois Press.

Nelson, G. (1987). *The Development of a Mental Health Coalition: An Action Research Project*. A poster presentation at the first biennial conference on community research and action, Columbia, South Carolina.

Nelson, R. (1987). Books, boredom, and behind bars: an explanation of apathy and hostility in our schools. In Wotherspoon, T., ed. *The Political Economy of Canadian Schooling*. Toronto: Methuen.

Oakley, A. (1981). Interviewing women: a contradiction in terms. In Roberts, H., ed. *Doing Feminist Research*. London: Routledge and Kegan Paul.

Ondaatje, M. (1992). *The English Patient*. Toronto: McClelland and Stewart.

Ontario. (1987). Evaluation Committee for the Psychiatric Patient Advocate Office. *Advocacy in Psychiatric Hospitals: Evaluation of the Psychiatric Patient Advocate Office*. Toronto: Ministry of Health.

Ontario. (1988). The Provincial Community Mental Health Committee. *Building Community Support for People: A Plan for Mental Health in Ontario*. Toronto: Ministry of Health.

Ontario. (1989). *District Health Councils: Partners in Health Planning*. Toronto: Ministry of Health.

Ontario. (1990a). The Legislative Sub-Committee of the Steering Committee on the Implementation of the Report of the Provincial Community Mental Health Committee. *Discussion Paper Towards Community Mental Health Services legislation*. Toronto: Ministry of Health.

Ontario. (1990b). The Implementation Strategy Sub-Committee of the Steering Committee on the Implementation of the Report of the Provincial Community Mental Health Committee. *Fitting the Pieces Together: Working Document for 'Building Community Support For People; A Plan for Mental Health in Ontario.'* Toronto: Ministry of Health.

Ontario Psychiatric Survivors Alliance. (May 1990). *OPSA Newsletter 1*.

Ontario Psychiatric Survivors Alliance. (November 1990). *OPSAnews 2*.

Ontario Psychiatric Survivors Alliance. (March 1991). *OPSAnews 3*.

Ontario Psychiatric Survivors Alliance. (June 1991). *OPSAnews 4*.

Ontario Psychiatric Survivors Alliance. (September 1991). *OPSAnews 5*.

Ontario Psychiatric Survivors Alliance. (January 1992). *OPSAnews 6*.

Ontario Psychiatric Survivors Alliance. (April 1992). *OPSAnews 7*.

Orr, J. (1990). Theory on the market: panic, incorporating. *Social Problems*, 37(4), 460–482.

Paget, M. (1990). Life mirrors work mirrors text mirrors life... *Social Problems*, 37(2), 137–148.

Pape, B. (1988). *Consumer Participation: From Concept to Reality*. Toronto: Canadian Mental Health Association (National).

Pape, B., and Church, K. (1987). *Community Reinvestment: Balancing the Use of Resources to Support People with Mental Disabilities*. Toronto: Canadian Mental Health Association (National).

Parkdale Activity and Recreation Centre. (1991). *Kiss Me You Mad Fool.* Toronto: Ontario Ministry of Health.

Peters, E. (1993). Table talk. In Haddad, T., and Lam, L., eds. *Reconstructing Canadian Men and Masculinities*. Toronto: Canadian Scholars Press.

Pettigrew, J. (1981). Reminiscences of fieldwork among the Sikhs. In Roberts, H., ed. *Doing Feminist Research*. London: Routledge and Kegan Paul.

Phillips, S. (1986). Some functions of spatial positioning and alignment in the organization of courtroom discourse. In Fisher, S., and Todd, A., eds. *Discourse and Institutional Authority: Medicine, Education, and Law.* Norwood, NJ: Ablex.

Porter, C. (1936). *I've Got You Under My Skin*. New York: Chappell and Co. Inc.

Reinharz, S. (1988). What's missing in miscarriage? *Journal of Community Psychology*, 16, 84–103.

Reville, D. (1967). From my side of the blue. *Gavel*. Kingston: Queen's University.

Reville, D. (1981). Don't spyhole me. *Phoenix Rising*, 2(1), special insert.

Reville, D. (1984). Don't spyhole me. *Kingston Whig Standard*.

Reville, D. (1987). *Breaking the Cycle*. Notes for a speech to the annual conference of the Canadian Hospital Association held in Vancouver, B.C.

Reville, D. (1988). Don't spyhole me. In Burstow, B., and Weitz, D., eds. *Shrink Resistant: The Struggle Against Psychiatry in Canada*. Vancouver: New Star Books.

Reville, D. (1990). *The Politics of Mental Health (A Speech You Can Eat With a Fork)*. Notes for a speech to the Luna Circle, a study group on the history of mental health in Canada, New College, University of Toronto.

Reville, D. (1991). *The Politics of Mental Health in Ontario: A Strategic Planning Framework for the Mental Health Facilities Branch of the Ontario Ministry of Health*. Available from David Reville, Special Advisor to the Premier, Queen's Park, Toronto.

Reville, D., and Church, K. (1990). *Do the Right Thing* Right*. A brief presented to the Toronto hearings of the legislative sub-committee on community mental health services legislation.

Rockhill, K. (1987). The chaos of subjectivity in the ordered halls of academe. *Canadian Woman Studies*, 8(4), 12–17.

Rogers, A., and Pilgrim, D. (1991). 'Pulling down churches': accounting for the British mental health users' movement. *Sociology of Health and Illness*, 13(2), 129–148.

Rosaldo, R. (1989). *Culture and Truth: The Remaking of Social Analysis*. Boston: Beacon Press.

Rose, S., and Black, B. (1985). *Advocacy and Empowerment: Mental Health Care in the Community*. Boston: Routledge and Kegan Paul.

Rosenberg, S. (1990). *Voices of a Struggling Subject*. Unpublished paper.

Roth, J. (1963). *Timetables: Structuring the Passage of Time in Hospital Treatment and Other Careers*. New York: Bobbs-Merrill.

Rothman, B. (1986). Reflections: on hard work. *Qualitative Sociology*, 9(1), 48–53.

Savage, H., and McKague, C. (1988). *Mental Health Law in Canada*. Toronto: Butterworths.

Schneider, J. (1991). Troubles with textual authority in sociology. *Symbolic Interaction*, 14(3), 295–319.

Shilling, C. (1992). Reconceptualizing structure and agency in the sociology of education: structuration theory and schooling. *British Journal of Sociology of Education*, 13(1), 69–87.

Silverstein, M. (1977). The history of a short, unsuccessful, academic career (with a postscript update). In Snodgrass, J., ed. *A Book of Readings: For Men Against Sexism*. New York: Times Change Press.

Simmons, H. (1990). *Unbalanced: Mental Health Policy in Ontario, 1930–1989*. Toronto: Wall and Thompson.

Simon, R. (1992). *Teaching Against the Grain: Texts for a Pedagogy of Possibility*. Toronto: OISE Press.

Slinger, J. (1990). Pleas, tears and profanity in a brave try for dignity. *Toronto Star*, Sunday, September 2, 1990.

Smith, D., and David, S., eds. (1975). *Women Look at Psychiatry*. Vancouver: Press Gang.

Smith, D. (1987). *The Everyday World as Problematic: A Feminist Sociology*. Boston: Northeastern University Press.

Smith, D. (1990). *Conceptual Practices of Power: A Feminist Sociology of Knowledge*. Toronto: University of Toronto Press.

Smith, D. (1991). Writing women's experience into social science. *Feminism and Psychology*, 1(1), 155–169.

Smith, D. (1992). Whistling women: reflections on rage and rationality. In Carroll, W., Christiansen-Ruffman, L., Currie, R., and Harrison, D., eds. *Fragile Truths: Twenty-Five Years of Sociology and Anthropology in Canada*. Ottawa: Carleton University Press.

Smith, G. (1990). Political activist as ethnographer. *Social Problems*, 37(4), 629–648.

Smith, P. (1988). *Discerning the Subject*. Minneapolis: University of Minnesota Press.

Smith, S. (1993). Who's talking/who's talking back? the subject of personal narrative. *Signs*, Winter, 393–407.

Spelman, E. (1989). Anger and insubordination. In Garry, A., and Pearsall, M., eds. *Women, Knowledge and Reality: Explorations in Feminist Philosophy*. Boston: Unwin Hyman.

Spence, J. (1990). Could do better ... "Towards a personal and political theatre of the self? *Practice*, 7(3), 24–27.

Spivak, G. (1987). *In Other Worlds: Essays in Cultural Politics*. New York: Methuen.

Stanley, L., and Wise, S. (1983). 'Back into the personal' or: our attempt to construct 'feminist research.' In Bowles, G., and Duelli Klein, R., eds. *Theories of Women's Studies*. London: Routledge and Kegan Paul.

Steedman, C. (1986). *Landscape for a Good Woman: A Story of Two Lives*. London: Virago.

Steinberg, D. (1977). *Father Journal: Five Years of Awakening to Fatherhood*. New York: Times Change Press.

Stivers, C. (1993). Reflections on the role of personal narrative in social science. *Signs*, Winter, 408–425.

Symth, J., ed. (1987). *Educating Teachers: Changing the Nature of Pedagogical Knowledge*. Philadelphia: Falmer Press.

Trainor, J., and Church, K. (1984). *A Framework for Support for People with Severe Mental Disabilities*. Toronto: Canadian Mental Health Association (National).

University of California At Berkeley. (1992). *Ask the Experts. Wellness Letter*, 8(4), 8.

Van Mannen, J. (1988). *Tales of the Field: On Writing Ethnography*. Chicago: University of Chicago Press.

Waitzkin, H. (1983). *The Second Sickness: Contradictions of Capitalist Health Care*. New York: Free Press.

Walkerdine, V. (1985). Dreams from an ordinary childhood. In Heron, L., ed. *Truth, Dare or Promise: Girls Growing Up in the Fifties*. London: Virago.

Walkerdine, V. (1987). Surveillance, subjectivity and struggle: lessons from domestic and pedagogic practice. *Occasional Paper #11*, Centre for Human Studies, University of Minnesota.

Warner, M. (1981). The rise of community participation: its impact on health professionals and the health bureaucracy. In Coburn, D., D'Arcy, C., New, P., and Torrance, G., eds. *Health and Canadian Society*. Don Mills: Fitzhenry and Whiteside.

Weedon, C. (1987). *Feminist Practice and Post-Structuralist Theory*. Oxford: Basil Blackwell.

Weitz, D. (1984). "On our own:" a self-help model. In Lumsden, D.P., ed. *Community Mental Health Action*. Ottawa: Canadian Public Health Association.

White, E.B. (1990). The door. In Mangual, A., ed. *Black Water 2: More Tales of the Fountain*. Toronto: Lester and Orpen Dennys.

Wilson, S. (1986). *An Analysis of the Mental Health Ex-Patient Movement in Vermont*. A dissertation presented to the Faculty of the Graduate College of the University of Vermont.

Woolgar, S. (1988). Reflexivity is the ethnographer of the text. In Woolgar, S., ed. *Knowledge and Reflexivity: New Frontiers in the Sociology of Knowledge*. London: Sage.

Woolgar, S. (1989). The ideology of representation and the role of the agent. Lawson H., and Appignanesi, L., eds. *Dismantling Truth: Reality in the Post-Modern World*. New York: St. Martin's Press.

Woolgar, S., and Ashmore, M. (1988)). The next step: an introduction to the reflexive project. In Woolgar, S., ed. *Knowledge and Reflexivity: New Frontiers in the Sociology of Knowledge*. London: Sage.

Zola, I. (1982). *Missing Pieces: A Chronicle of Living with a Disability*. Philadelphia: Temple University Press.

Zola, I. (1991). Bringing our bodies and ourselves back in: reflections on a past, present and future "medical sociology." *Journal of Health and Social Behavior*, 32, 1–16.

INDEX

A

Academia, 21–23, 37–39

Action research, 24

Activist research, 141, 142

Advocacy and psychiatric
survivors, 25

Alice in Wonderland syndrome,
136–137

Alternative medicine, 129–132

Anger
expression of, 105–106
self-directed, 58

Antibiotic poisoning, 134

B

Behavior, definition of proper,
82–85

Behavioral code, 90–93

Breakdown, emotional, 52–61,
64–65

C

Canadian Mental Health
Association (CMHA), 1,
16–19, 23, 32

Capponi, Pat, 24–27, 54–55,
66–67

Community Mental Health
Branch, 119

Community services, 6

Consumer participation, 1–2, 5–6,
12–13, 19, 47, 51–52, 74–94,
111–112, 116

Consumer/Survivor Development
Initiative, 119, 122–123

Consumers/survivors, 23–24
and relationship with mental
health professionals, 66–69,
73–113, 140
and research, 42
and self–help, 36–37
attitudes, 141–142
development of, 117–120
emotional constraints, 106–107
participation, redefinition of,
73–74
relating to, 64–65

Critical autobiography, 3, 4, 5

D

Decency, 108–109

Deinstitutionalization, 5

Drug toxicity, 58–59

E

Emotional socialization, 89–94

Emotional subjectivity, 54–55

157

SOCIAL SCIENCE LIBRARY

Oxford University Library Services
Manor Road
Oxford OX1 3UQ
Tel: (2)71093 (enquiries and renewals)
http://www.ssl.ox.ac.uk

This is a NORMAL LOAN item.

We will email you a reminder before this item is due.

Please see http://www.ssl.ox.ac.uk/lending.html
for details on:

- loan policies; these are also displayed on the notice boards and in our library guide.

- how to check when your books are due back.

- how to renew your books, including information on the maximum number of renewals. Items may be renewed if not reserved by another reader. Items must be renewed before the library closes on the due date.

- level of fines; fines are charged on overdue books.

Please note that this item may be recalled during Term.